NEW TECHNIQUES
FOR EFFECTIVE
SCHOOL ADMINISTRATION

NEW TECHNIQUES
FOR EFFECTIVE
SCHOOL ADMINISTRATION

Norman K. Hamilton

Parker Publishing Company, Inc.   West Nyack, N.Y.

Library of Congress Cataloging in Publication Data

Hamilton, Norman K
  New techniques for effective school administration.

  Includes bibliographical references and index.
  1. School management and organization. I. Title.
LB2805.H27   371.2   75-19246
ISBN 0-13-615922-2

ABOUT THE AUTHOR

Norman K. Hamilton is Director of the Curriculum Development Programs Division at the Northwest Regional Educational Laboratory in Portland, Oregon. His long standing interest in the improvement of the decision-making process as a means of improving educational programs in the public schools has led to this book.

After receiving his Ed.D. at Stanford University in general administration, he was both teacher and administrator in small and large school systems as well as visiting professor of administration and instruction at several colleges and universities. A major portion of his professional experience was applied to his position as assistant superintendent of the Portland, Oregon, public schools.

Dr. Hamilton has served on several national committees and commissions which have led to publications with NEA, ASCD, and AASA. He has also contributed numerous articles to national educational journals.

The Scope & Practical Value of This Book

The chapters that follow present the best of new school management techniques carefully selected to assist the experienced administrator in his search for administrative excellence. Few of us can afford administrative failures, especially in these days of fast-moving events and conflicting pressures from teachers, students and the community we serve.

As you proceed through this book you will learn how to do a needs assessment to determine those things which will make a positive difference in your school system. You will be able to apply the "triad technique" to involve more people in decision making and thus gain their commitment, and you will discover how to use resolution techniques that generate solutions for groups with purposes which are often diametrically opposed.

In a real sense, this book can become a handbook for immediate and continued reference. For example, when applications of flow charting or PPBS are indicated, you can use the book as valuable resource information on the specific details of the processes and to utilize the detailed aids and suggestions included in the chapters.

ADMINISTRATIVE PROBLEM SOLVING SKILLS

These problem solving approaches have been identified by practicing administrators as the most useful to them of the many available. Specifically, they will help you learn to:

1. Improve your efficiency by:

Selecting more carefully those things to which you give personal attention through goal selection and establishing priorities.

Coordinating your activities to build successively toward a specific goal to be achieved through the application of flow charting approaches and PPBS technology.

2. Improve your effectiveness by:

Assuring success from the beginning by the use of force field analysis which will also help in considering the human concerns that are so important to those affected by your decisions.

3. Make your accountability evident by:

Making evident the orderly procedure used in reaching your decisions through the use of decision matrices.

Guaranteeing that consideration has been given to the total impact of the decisions you reach by systematically considering the elements that must go into every important decision.

4. Enhance the credibility in your administrative role by:

Reducing administrative errors through planning and consideration of data provided by the new emerging "futures projections."

Making your competence as a problem solver visible to others through use of the modified Delphi approaches supported by other consensus approaches.

5. Improve communication by:

Involving each group at the proper time and in the proper manner as problems are being solved. The appropriate roles and functions of the public, the professionals and students alike in selecting courses of action are explained and illustrated.

Selecting systematically those persons who must be kept informed of actions contemplated or taken by use of effective public relations approaches.

These and other more specific skills can be accomplished by utilizing many of the sample instruments in your schools and by following the simple steps in the processes presented.

ADMINISTRATIVE LEADERSHIP

This book will not only help you as a decision maker, but will help you develop plans and innovations which are failsafe. It will guide your development of leadership competencies and help you select many of the new, *tested* instructional systems to build staff competencies in such things as effective communications skills, teaching strategies and problem solving.

The knotty problems associated with a decentralized, local and autonomous organization structure are covered in specific detail. Essential conditions for such a system to be successful are spelled out. The whole area of accountability is presented with appropriate techniques for staff analysis and determination of milestone review points.

CUMULATIVE SKILL DEVELOPMENT

In an easily understood and nontechnical manner, the book presents authentic, tested approaches. Individual techniques are presented, each independent and self-sufficient. Combined, however, they provide you with a repertoire of powerful new methods for working constructively toward successful administrative problem solving.

The presentations are cumulative in effect. First, each technique is thoroughly explained and applied to successive situations, some more complex than others. The examples have been selected for their practical value. Each section includes possible reactions to be anticipated and planned for in the application of these processes. Each chapter takes you step by step through the processes presented so you can acquire a clear understanding of the technique and the *skill* necessary to apply it.

The techniques selected are directly related to a needs assessment conducted among practicing school administrators. Those administrators surveyed rated by priority the following categories of needs: goals and objectives development; priority setting techniques; problem analysis; Planning, Programming, Budgeting Systems (PPBS); cost analysis; Program Evaluation Review Technique (PERT) and Critical Path Method (CPM); issue analysis; survey techniques; flow charting; public relations; supervisory processes and conflict management. Accordingly, these topics and more are included and organized into their logical relationships.

With the background of understanding and technical skill presented in this book, you as an administrator will have at your disposal a collection of effective methods for reliable, data-based decision making. As a result you will become not only more self-sufficient in your own ability to solve problems, but also in building the confidence of others who depend upon your leadership. You will always be able to make your decisions explicit and to clearly identify the rational methods used in arriving at them.

Norman K. Hamilton

Contents

NEW TECHNIQUES
FOR EFFECTIVE
SCHOOL ADMINISTRATION

1

How to Relate New Management Techniques to the Decision-Making Process

Educators at every level in the school system are necessarily decision makers. Their work calls for the exercise of judgment and the use of discretion in the everchanging combinations of circumstances which surround them.

Intelligent decision making requires an evaluative attitude on the part of the decision makers toward every dimension of the decision-making process. Various kinds of beliefs (theories and philosophical outlooks), as well as information (scientific data and informal observations), along with a whole host of purposes, values and assumptions go into the process. All of these elements are present and necessary in a sound decision process. All are equally important and interrelated. What one believes, along with the data he uses in making a decision, can be subjected to the same kinds of systematic analysis. In order to explain or defend one's behavior as a decision maker, one must understand the processes he has used and the elements which have influenced his decisions.

One might ask why the process of decision is discussed first when this book is about new techniques for effective school administration. Techniques are essentially ways of doing things and connote skill in using tools, instruments and systematic processes. Most of the techniques included in this book are specific, but are applied within the context of broad problem areas and concerns.

A technique presented in isolation or outside a conceptual framework is a barren thing. For example, the technique of using a triad to assure fuller participation, or the technique of using perception checking to assure accuracy in meaning, both take on broader meaning if each is shown within the context of a real problem-solving situation.

In a broader sense, systematic organization of ideas is also a technique. These are the methods for logically organizing the elements that go into the decision process so that we know all the dimensions that should be considered before we begin to apply specific techniques. Therefore, this particular chapter looks at the systematic elements that are important to the process, while others will zero in more specifically on the specific techniques themselves. The two go hand in hand to strengthen the reader's decision processes.

Most of us admire a decisive person, one who puts an end to our doubts. We especially want this in persons to whom we look for leadership. On the other hand, we like a person who is fair to all concerned and in whom we can put our confidence to make wise decisions. If we get the feeling that decisions which affect us are based upon capricious or arbitrary action, we lose faith in that leadership. The best of all combinations is careful decisiveness—based upon sound data which we, too, can understand, sound values which we share and systematic deliberations in which we have had a part.

Decisions and prerogative: Who has the right in the school system to make which decisions? Conventions dictate certain expectations regarding who participates at what level of decision making. Generally, certain categories of decisions are left to the Board of Education, others to the superintendent, others to principals, supervisors, teachers and even clerical personnel. Circumstances sometimes change these expectations, yet generally each category of personnel has expectations regarding who can make the final decision about what.

Joe Ward was the superintendent of a moderate sized school system. He studied carefully the financial situation and made several judgments. The operational budget was tight, while the building fund had uncommitted money. Should Joe transfer money from the building fund to the operational budget in order to run the schools without a deficit?

Clearly, Joe was out of his area of prerogative. The decision simply was not his to make. It was proper for him to make the analysis and to consider alternatives, but both legal and conventional considerations indicated that the prerogative to make the decision was with the Board of Education in the areas of budget transfer and possibly the state legislature, if the law did not permit transfer of sums from capital expenditures to operations.

Let's look at another case involving Janet Caldwell, a principle of a Washington elementary school. She believed strongly that a nongraded organization in the primary grades would improve instruction. Should Janet reorganize her primary department into a nongraded plan for next year?

Janet was within the general bounds of her prerogative to organize her school according to the educational needs of the children. On the other hand, convention (usual procedure) demanded that the decision be shared as a collegial decision with her staff and that it be sanctioned by others in the school system who shared responsibility with her. Further, she would be expected to involve the parents to gain acceptance of the whole plan since it is a severe departure from their current expectations.

Thus we see two examples of where prerogative plays an important part in the decision process. The five elements of prerogative which must be considered are:

1. Convention: The usual processes used to meet expectation of who has the right to make the decision.
2. Legal: The laws concerning the decision.
3. Collegial: The general expectation on the part of members of the organization to participate in the process.
4. Sanction: The extent to which a decision maker requires the approval of others in the organization who share accountability.
5. Readiness: The degree of expectation held by those affected.

Values and decisions: We have all heard the oft-quoted truism from Dewey that a theory is a very practical thing. Philosophy, theory and a value system are all interrelated. Each has a precise definition, but for our purpose I will group them together as values, the things we believe in. Throughout the eleven chapters which follow, values are consistently referred to as important elements in the systematic selection and application of techniques.

Joe Ward, as superintendent, got a complaint about a teacher in an elementary school who had applied corporal punishment to a seven year old child. He told the parents that obviously the child had needed the spanking, that the authority of the school was at stake and that such a procedure was legal. The unhappy parents were dismissed. Here Joe's values came to the fore. He valued the authority of the school. He valued the support of staff and had a commitment to supporting them, right or wrong.

Alternative values would have caused him to make other decisions. If he had valued due process he would have told the parents that he would investigate the matter thoroughly and talk to the teacher before he made a decision. If he had valued the psychological well-being of children most highly, he would have been concerned as to what effect the spanking had on the child and would have approached the problem differently. If, on the other hand, he had valued parents' goodwill toward the school most highly, he would have assured the parent of satisfaction by reprimanding the teacher. Joe should think through his value system regarding these kinds of incidents so that he can avoid having to grasp for an expedient solution in the future. If he clarifies his values and develops a theory or philosophy, it will be a great convenience to him later on. He can then defend his position to all concerned and be assured that his decision was the best he could make.

Janet Caldwell, the elementary principal, had a problem with her first- and second-grade teachers. The situation had developed because of an increase in enrollment which necessitated the addition of a split section consisting of the overflow of 12 first graders and 12 second graders. The establishment of this combination section was to occur the second week of school. A beginning teacher had been sent over from the superintendent's office. Each experienced teacher had selected the children to be transferred to the new room, and each expected to keep her regular class minus the overflow. The inexperienced teacher would then have the most difficult teaching situation, consisting of two grades compounded by what Janet suspected was the "dumping" of some problem children into the new room by the older teachers.

The alternative decisions available to Janet were:

1. Assign the new teacher to the new room, and keep quiet and see how things go.
2. Transfer an experienced teacher to the new room and accept the teacher's unhappiness.
3. Reconstruct the new class to consist of a manageable group with no problem children.

If Janet valued the idea of seniority of the existing staff, she would have selected alternative one. If she valued the children's educational progress most, she would have probably selected a combination of alternatives two and three. If she valued the smooth introduction of a new staff member into the profession, she would have selected alternative two.

Here, Janet not only needed to sort out her values but she also needed some techniques for negotiation among the staff.

These two examples were selected to illustrate the role of values in the decision-making process. They are the criteria against which we test possible solutions to problems according to our beliefs.

Clarified values are important to decision because:

1. They provide us with a convenient point of reference against which to test the soundness of solutions to problems.
2. They are always there when we need them, and we don't have to grasp for an expedient solution.
3. They lend a consistency to our decisions which is visible to others.
4. They permit us to explain our decisions to others.

Data and decisions: We all need information to make wise decisions. Whether or not we have authentic data, we still act as if we had when we make decisions. Data are at several levels on a continuum from pure guessing on the one hand to authenticated data on the other. Usually, we have to work somewhere in between. But the closer we can come to authenticated data, the better off we are. Our data consist of statistics, perceptions and assumptions. All can be valid and all must be mixed together to form a judgment on the part of the decision maker. Many of the new breed in education appear to value only the quantifiable data, that which can be put on a chart. The wise old heads in school administration temper these data with perceptions, hopefully checked, and assumptions on how things ought to be, hopefully accurate.

Other chapters will provide specific techniques for perception checking, validating assumptions and moderating statistics with judgment. But here, we are concerned with the role of data in the decision process.

Again, let's look at the kind of decision Joe Ward as superintendent must make. He was required to project the population growth for his district before preparing the budget. Joe looked at the current school population by grade and moved them up one year—a straight line projection. He then estimated the incoming class based on last year's enrollment and added up the figures. Since he did not make an error in arithmetic, the data were statistically accurate and chartable.

If Joe had made his projection on these data alone, would it be sound? Maybe so and maybe not. Other sources of data should include a review of building permits, the number of new telephone customers, the birth rate five years before in local hospitals, the potential removal of houses for a new freeway and the industrial situation which provided employment in the community.

Joe needed not only accurate data in each category, but he needed multiple sources of data tempered with judgment, perceptions and wise guesses.

Another source of good, valid data is not quantitative at all. They are purely subjective, but they can be as accurate as statistical data. These are the opinions and beliefs of people affected by decisions. Remember the case of Janet Caldwell and her wish to start a nongraded primary. The degree to which this innovation will be accepted may be determined only by checking her own perception of how people will feel about it and whether or not she can influence or change attitudes of those who might oppose the decision.

If Janet were actually going to pursue such a program, she would need to apply several techniques for checking her guesses and assumptions. At that time, the sources of data available to her were few—only her perceptions of the way people felt about her idea. She needed to identify some opinion leaders in both parents and faculty to search out their feelings on the matter, which would have given her a clue to how much support she could count on. She needed to do some tentative opinion surveys in order to ascertain how far apart her ideas were from prevailing opinions.

There are, of course, many more things Janet will need to do before a nongraded primary program can be installed. But for now, she had enough data to help her decide whether or not to pursue the idea at that time and what course of action to take in the future.

Data for decision making should meet the following criteria:

1. They should be as accurate as possible.
2. They should be from several sources. One source may be entirely accurate but inadequate for the decision purpose.
3. They should be tempered with wisdom. All data must be put into judgmental perspective because with few exceptions no single source of data can stand alone as a basis for decision.
4. Subjective data are valid for decision making. The requirement here is that they must be validated by checking.

Influence and decisions: Our American folkways support the image of the fearless, self-sufficient leader. This is the person who stands against the multitudes and moves ahead courageously against all odds when he believes he is right. This is an erroneous concept of good leadership. All of us are influenced by others and in turn influence others. The more secure and self-reliant we are, the more we will seek out and accept positive influence. If we clearly understand the place of influence in our decision process and the frequent need for it, we can increase the efficiency of our efforts and be more innovative and productive.

Joe Ward had been offered a new position in a larger school system. He had completed only three years in his present position and felt he was just ready to make great strides. He had the confidence of his Board, and they had just approved his recommendation for a new high school which Joe would have liked to have the experience of building. Joe also liked fishing in the area.

On the other hand, Joe was ambitious in his profession. The offer would have given him new challenge, new recognition as a comer, not to mention a better salary. It also would have presented some risks. The district which sought him out had money problems, teacher union problems and an obsolete school plant. Joe had recently read that young superintendents who move after a reasonable time tend to keep moving, while those who are "place bound" tend to remain so.

Who will Joe let influence him in his decision? Certainly he will discuss it with his wife and family. He may even talk it over with trusted friends and colleagues.

Joe made his decision after he called one of his admired former professors at the university. The professor said, "Joe, I can't tell you what decision to make. I can tell you that this new position is highly sought after. If you want to break into a major city as superintendent, this is one of the better spots. It is my opinion that this is the time for you to move if this is what you want."

Joe was influenced, and he did move.

At another level, Janet Caldwell was called into the superintendent's office and offered another principalship in the same school district. Janet would not get a raise in salary because she was already at the maximum. She also knew that she could not be required to move because of seniority. The other school was more difficult and in a poorer neighborhood, and the opportunity for her to realize her dream of starting a nongraded primary would be remote.

The superintendent said, "Janet, I have decided that you should move to this other school because we need you there. A less experienced and less able principal can handle your present school. You have high professional dedication which I recognize and therefore I know you will accept this new assignment and not cause me to re-evaluate my opinion of your professional dedication."

Janet was influenced and moved.

In these two examples, we see two different kinds of influence. One was open and noncompulsory. The other was closed and a directive. Janet simply did not have a choice unless she wanted to defy her superintendent and suffer the results of a poor relationship.

There are still other levels of influence, such as the collegial influence that goes into a group decision where the opinion of each person is sought out and respected.

The dimension here is that influence is indeed important to the decision process. One must decide to what extent he will seek out or submit to influence.

Influence is an important consideration because:

1. We are all influenced by others and should be aware of it.
2. Sometimes we can control the degree of influence we let others exert upon us and our decision process.
3. Sometimes influence is exerted in such a manner as to cut off our decision process and force us into a decision dictated by others.
4. Influence can be a positive or negative force.

Decision and negotiation: Most of us in school work would like to believe that we can eventually reach a satisfactory solution to most school problems. This is a false dream. Some objectives are so diametrically opposite each other that the expectation of a solution satisfactory to each party is not possible. In this case the decision must be a negotiated one in which both parties win something but give up something. The most obvious application of negotiation in the school situation is teacher salary and welfare negotiations, which are now the pattern throughout the United States.

Negotiation should also be recognized at other levels in the school situation. It is the process which .must be used with any face to face conflict situation.

Joe Ward found that conflict resolution (negotiation) played an ever more important role in his decision process. For example, he received a court order to desegregate his inner city school which was almost totally black. The parents of surrounding schools objected to busing and stated in no uncertain terms that they wanted a "neighborhood" school. Joe had to make a decision about what course of action to follow. It had to be a negotiated one because any other resolution would not succeed. The negotiated solution in this case resulted in the establishment of an early childhood center in the formerly mostly black school and the distribution of the other three grades to neighboring schools. The districts were redrawn to pie-shaped districts so that all schools had approximately 20 percent black children and 80 percent white.

This negotiated position gave everyone something, yet no one got everything he wanted. The gains for the neighborhood school group were (1) opportunity for their children to be bused into an early childhood center offering kindergarten where it was not offered before; (2) retaining the major part of their school in their neighborhood.

The black community gained by (1) having children come into their neighborhood for a better and more innovative early childhood program than they had before, and (2) a reduced amount of busing to only half the elementary grades for their children.

In the case of Janet, we see another level of conflict. In this case, the local PTA had traditionally sponsored a school carnival. The children liked it. The PTA leaders took it on as their major project for the year and it proved to be an important rallying point for neighborhood identity and social interchange.

The faculty resisted the carnival idea. Each carnival had become more elaborate than the one before. The year before, the school had been denied the use of the gym and cafeteria for a week ahead and almost a week after the event. Children had been overexcited and hard to teach. Also, each room tended to compete with others to sell the most tickets for the carnival. The teachers decided that this year they would not go along with the carnival idea.

The decision was Janet's, and she negotiated the following solutions: The parents got a school event but at a greatly reduced scale. It was turned into an open house with refreshments served in the cafeteria and children's contests and games in the gymnasium. The teachers gained something. They got a modified activity that was more educationally sound and less demanding on the children's time and their own workload.

Each lost something, as was pointed out.

Negotiation is important to the decision process when unresolvable conflict exists.

1. Negotiation results in some gains and some losses to each party.
2. Negotiation brings both parties into the decision process.
3. Negotiation requires the moderation of the decision maker with the ultimate purpose of resolving the conflict into an acceptable situation in which neither party loses totally.

Evaluation: No discussion of the decision-making process in the public schools would be complete without the inclusion of evaluation as a process. Whether evaluation is a dimension of the decision-making process or a separate process is an academic question. Certainly each decision has or should have elements of evaluation in it. But in the broader sense, evaluation is a process of measuring or appraising the value or worth of a thing. It therefore seems to be a process separate from, but important to, the decision process.

Evaluation specialists are not in strict agreement as to whether or not systematic evaluation includes the generation of the final decision that the evidence supports. There is little doubt on the part of administrators that evaluation generates data, but does not include decision making. This means that the decision which results from systematic appraisal of a program for the purpose of collecting and organizing information can be used for the final decision by the accountable person.

Systematic evaluation of programs within the public school setting has not been a high-priority process in most school systems. It is receiving much more attention now than it did a few years ago, partly because of the emphasis that has been put upon it by the guidelines of federally funded programs. Many school systems do not have sufficient staff to meet these requirements and have therefore contracted with outside specialists to do their appraisals for them.

Evaluation should be an ongoing part of any problem-solving process or program being developed. It can contribute most when it is established at the beginning of any undertaking for which pertinent information is needed along the way. The steps which must be included in any evaluation process include at least the following:

1. The enumeration of the goals, objectives and/or standards for the program.
2. The designation of information essential to compare the performance with the goals, objectives and/or standards for the program.

3. The design of instruments or other methods of collecting the data desired.
4. The identification of the discrepancies between what is desired and what exists. (The extension of these discrepancies into theories of causation would logically be a part of this identification process.)
5. The indication of what corrective action should be taken to lessen or eliminate the discrepancy.

This process leads to the brink of the decision, but it does not generate the decision itself. It does, however, speculate as to what needs to be done. The decision maker is the person who has the responsibility for the decision. Usually this is a different level of administration than that which is held by the evaluator.

When this process is applied along the way, it is called *formative* evaluation. Formative evaluation is to assure good and immediate information to assist a project or program director in making good decisions along the way. The better the formative evaluation, the better the end result will be.

When the process is applied only at the end of a project or program it is *summative* evaluation—that which summarizes the results and leads to a three-alternative decision:

Decisions

Summative evaluation data ——————
$\Big\{$
Eliminate the program as not meeting the objectives

Recycle the program with corrective measures

Continue the program as satisfactorily meeting the objectives

Joe Ward desired to lessen the dropout rate for the high schools of his district. He applied for and received Title III funds to improve the counseling program in order to help potential dropouts to solve some of their personal problems and select alternative, meaningful educational experiences. Joe worked with his project directors to ascertain the needed formative data. The questions he needed answered included:

1. What were the major causes of dropouts over the last five years?
2. What is the best way of identifying potential dropouts?
3. What counseling services do potential dropouts need?
4. What alternative programs should we offer potential dropouts?
5. What changes in our present program are needed?

These above questions, if answered through formative data, would produce many theories based upon information.

1. Information: Most dropouts didn't see any purpose in what they were studying.

   Theory: "Potential dropouts will respond to school better if they see immediate application to their lives of what they were studying."

2. Information: Most dropouts in the past were boys at the sophomore and junior level who had failed two or more classes.

   Theory: "The best way to identify potential dropouts would be to look at the failure in the ninth grade."

3. Information: Most dropouts said they hadn't ever seen the counselor except when they were sent there for disciplinary action.

   Theory: "The counselor should not become the disciplinarian, but should be the advocate for the student."

4. Information: Most dropouts needed money and thought they didn't need a high school education to get a job. The $2.50 an hour they could get pumping gas looked awfully good.

   Theory: "Introduce a work-study program for those who needed money. Show them how their earnings could be improved if they increased their training."

5. Information: The most frequently failed class in school was the required sophomore English course which included *Julius Caesar* and the preparation of a term paper.

   Theory: "Most sophomore dropouts are not very good in English. An alternative course in communicative skills should be offered. These would deal with the practical aspects of speaking, listening, reading and writing, and would center on the interests of the students."

In the above five examples, we see the role of formative evaluation to help the decision maker along the way. At this stage in the project, data were needed to help the project director prepare theories to be tried. He might have been able from experience to guess these things, but they would have been guesses with a much higher risk of failure than if they were based on sound data. Also, teachers, reviewers and colleagues in the project would certainly be more willing to go along with the program if they, too, were convinced the theories were good ones and based on good information.

Janet Caldwell had introduced an alternative reading program three years ago. The reading program had three alternatives:

1. An integrated reading series traditionally used in most school systems.
2. A phonetic series based upon the classical phonetic approaches.
3. A linguistic series based upon the patterns of the language such as, "The rat sat on a mat."

Janet had had the assistance of an evaluation specialist in setting up the program and had followed the essentials for the experiment carefully.

1. She had divided the ninety-three entering first graders randomly into three groups.
2. She had let each teacher select the series she wanted to teach on the theory that a teacher would teach better with materials she wanted to use.
3. Each teacher had agreed to follow the program as advocated by its authors. The teacher did not, in other words, teach "off the top of her head."
4. Careful records were kept on many aspects of the program including pupil, teacher and parent satisfaction.
5. Janet had arranged with a fellow principal for some pupils in that school of like socioeconomic status to act as control subjects.

All of the ingredients of a fairly traditional evaluation design had been met. Therefore, the program was ready for its summative evaluation.

If these prior conditions had not been met, the summative evaluation would have been very difficult, possibly requiring some new experimentation.

In this case, Janet received the following summative results:

1. All of the classes did better than the control group.
2. Generally, overall achievements were about the same. Each class had its area wherein it did better than other classes, but the results when statistically tested were not highly significant.
3. Parents, teachers and pupils tended to favor and be highly satisfied with the approach they were using.

Janet then had the data needed to make the decision. She talked over the results with the teachers and parents, and thus shared her decisions with others even though she had the prerogative to make them herself. She also formulated the values most important to all concerned, i.e., that children should have the best program for them.

The data were then reviewed and each group was put into a position where they could influence the decision. Those conflicting views were talked out and negotiated.

The final decision was to let each teacher continue in the series she selected on the assumption that teachers do better if they can use the materials they like.

It was decided that parents could have some say about the approach their child would use.

It was also decided to encourage teachers to try new things on the assumption that teachers do better if they are exploring new approaches and ideas.

Janet could have come to other decisions with the same data. In this case, all elements of the decision process came into play, and each was carefully considered: prerogative—values—data—influence—negotiation. The whole process was made possible only by a careful summative evaluation study.

SUMMARY

As was pointed out earlier in this chapter, there is new technology to assist in the decision process. These techniques are best understood when presented within the problem-solving context. Systematic understanding of the dimensions of decision making is also a technology which permits the decision maker systematically to analyze his process and to make explicit to himself and others the values, data and other considerations that went into the decisions.

The chapter presented five dimensions of the decision-making process and gave two levels of examples to illustrate each. The dimensions presented were:

1. Prerogative, which answers the question, "Who has the right to make which decision?" The decision maker must consider the following:

   Convention: Indicating the usual process used.

   Legal restraints: Referring to the laws which may designate the decision makers.

   Sanction: The need for administrative approval of those who share accountability with the decision maker.

   Readiness: The state of preparation of those who will be most affected.

2. Values: Those theories, beliefs and philosophies which are important to us and against which we test our decisions. They should be evident in the decision process:

   To provide us with a point of reference against which to test soundness of decisions.

   To eliminate the need for an expedient solution.

   To lend consistency to our decisions.

   To permit us to explain our decisions.

3. Data: The information on which we base our decisions. They can be objective or subjective. Data should meet the following criteria:

Whether subjective or objective, they must be as accurate as possible.

Several diversified sources of data are better than one.

Data must be put into perspective and tempered with judgment.

Validity of subjective information should be tested.

4. Influence: The forces that others bring to bear on our decision process. Influence is an important consideration because:

We are all influenced by others to some degree.

Sometimes we can control the amount of influence we permit others to exert.

Sometimes influence is exerted in such a manner as to force a specific decision.

Influence can be a positive or negative force on our decision process.

5. Negotiation: The process used to resolve conflict to an acceptable compromise. Negotiation is important to the decision process because:

It results in each party making some gain and usually some loss.

It brings both parties into the decision process.

It requires the moderation of the accountable decision maker.

Evaluation: Evaluation is a process for the systematic measurement of the worth or desirability of a project or program. Evaluation is related to the decision process by providing systematically organized data. Two major categories of evaluation are a) *formative*—that which provides information upon which to base decisions during the process of developing a project or program and b) *summative*—that which provides information on which to assess the total effect of a project or program. It leads to the decisions which suggest elimination of the program because it does not meet expectations, recycling or redoing the project after making certain corrections, or to continue the program as satisfactory.

Generally, evaluation must assure that the following things have been accomplished:

1. That goals, objectives and standards have been defined.
2. That the information needed has been designated.
3. That the instruments and other procedures for getting the information have been designed.
4. That discrepancies, if any, between the desired results and the actual results have been identified.
5. That the corrective action, if needed, has been indicated.

2

Isolating the Problems and Making a Needs Assessment

Vice President Thomas R. Marshall,[1] while presiding over the Senate during a discussion of the country's needs, facetiously remarked, "What this country needs is a really good five cent cigar." The statement was catchy, had an element of humor and has therefore often been repeated, mainly during political campaigns. It is not taken as a serious needs assessment of the country, but rather serves to direct attention away from real or serious needs during a time of stressful political campaigning.

Everyone is constantly assessing his needs. When he intends to act on the assessment, he is conducting a needs assessment of sorts. Often it is not clear just what value system a decision maker is using when he makes a choice. Thus we have our teahouses in the August moon, our football stadiums and our new libraries. All of this happens because someone's concerns are screened through a set of values which determine choices. When this process is formalized, we have a systematic needs assessment.

If you ask a group of parents what their schools need, they most likely will head the list with "more discipline." This will be followed by other concerns such as better financing, better facilities or a more effective drug education program. On the other hand, school administrators will most often head the list with concerns for finance followed by integration-segregation issues. They will usually put school discipline in third or fourth place.

---

[1]Marshall was Vice President during the Wilson administration.

The Gallup polls[2] have listed the contrasting general concerns of parents and school personnel as follows:

PROBLEMS

Parents	Professional Educators
1. Discipline	1. Finances
2. Finances	2. Integration/Segregation
3. Integration/Segregation	3. Discipline
4. Teachers	4. Parents' lack of interest
5. Large schools, large classes	5. Large schools, large classes
6. Parents' lack of interest	6. Teachers
7. Facilities	7. Dope, drugs
8. Curriculum	8. Curriculum
9. Dope, drugs	9. Facilities

The Gallup poll illustrates the difference in the concerns of two categories of people (parents and school personnel). These expressions of concern are only the first step in the conduct of needs assessment. Such a list becomes a needs assessment when concerns are compared with the situation as it really is and when a difference or discrepancy is established between what is and what ought to be. A systematic needs assessment is therefore reduced to four major steps.

FOUR STEPS IN NEEDS ASSESSMENT

Identifying Areas of Concerns	Checking to Determine What Is	Clarifying Values or Criteria—What Ought to Be	Listing Discrepancies— Needs

Figure 2-1

You might ask, "Is all this necessary?" Don't we really know what the schools need and can't we rely on our own judgment of what is needed? The answer is, "Not necessarily." You will note that parents and school personnel do not agree upon the priority of needs. You might ask further, "Shouldn't the trained educator's judgment prevail because they are the professionals?" Again, the answer is, "Not necessarily." Most theorists agree that the public (society as a whole) should set the goals or policies for education while the professionals furnish the expertise on how to achieve the goals.

---

[2]George H. Gallup, "Fourth Annual Gallup Poll of Public Attitudes Toward Education," *Phi Delta Kappan*, Vol. LIV, No. 1 Sept. 1972, pp. 33-46.

Needs assessments can and should be conducted at all levels within the school system; at the classroom level, the individual school level, at the district level or at the state level.

The applications of needs assessment processes in the example which follows illustrates a consistent pattern of a systematic approach. In this example a new principal was assigned to a neighborhood middle school (grades 5-8). The district had been recently reorganized from a K8-4 plan into a (K-4) (5-8) (9-12) organization. The school had begun operation as a middle school (grades 5-8) with the former traditional curriculum and teaching methods. The school continued for three years with little attention given to the unique needs of the middle years child. Nor was there an analysis of the educational contributions which could be made through the new organization.

Parents and teachers were asking such questions as, "Why did we organize a middle school? Isn't it more costly? We don't see our children learning any more than they did in the old school."

This situation is more typical than not. Most reorganizations occur primarily as convenient administrative arrangements to solve immediate problems such as housing, busing or cost reduction efforts. Not always, but often, the educational benefits are left for later consideration.

The new principal in this situation was faced with the problem of giving leadership in making a plan which would achieve significant educational gain for the students in the school, and at the same time secure community support and lessen criticism. Through the process of preparing a needs assessment, he hoped to build understandings and elicit cooperation and commitment on the part of the community, the staff, the policy makers of the district and the students themselves, so that the plan to be evolved would be understood and attainable.

IDENTIFYING CONCERNS

The principal set about the task by involving all groups in the school system who had some level of involvement in the school. He wanted to begin collecting or "harvesting" their concerns, the first step in a needs assessment.

The faculty was the logical place to begin. Without their understanding of what was going on, anxieties would develop and the reaction would be withdrawal toward protecting themselves from exposure, or possibly open hostility. Honest expressions of concerns were essential. In this case, the principal simply listed on a chart in an open faculty meeting the first rough collection of concerns of the teachers without too much discussion. He displayed in every possible way assurances to teachers that their expressions were valued. To evaluate expressed concerns at this point would have cut off discussion and would have resulted in teachers carefully suggesting only those things which they were sure would meet approval.

Such obvious concerns as the following were stated:

Class size—we need smaller classes.

Better materials—we need more books and workbooks.

Better control—we need another vice principal to receive our discipline cases.

Better parent cooperation—we need assurances from parents that they will back the teacher and insist on children doing their homework.

More special teachers—we need a reading specialist who will give remedial instruction to children so that they can read the assignments we give them.

EXPANDING AND REFINING AREAS OF CONCERN
(Use of the triad technique)

At the second faculty meeting all of these suggestions, without too much editing or ordering and no identification of who said what, were distributed to the teachers on mimeographed sheets. By this time teachers had been thinking about their concerns and were ready to continue. Many teachers, however, were not ready to stand up in front of their colleagues and state their concerns. A small group technique for assuring more participation was used. The faculty was divided into *triads* with the assignment of looking at these concerns, restating them and adding to them. Each member of the triad was to do the following:

1. Each member of the triad, in turn, is to state a concern.
2. Each of the other two members, in turn, is to check his perception by *paraphrasing* the stated concern.
3. The first member then restates his concern as he wishes it stated.

General rules were:

a) In the perception checking, only rephrasing for clarification can be stated. No evaluative statements may be made.
b) This must be a helping situation. Each member is to help the stater of a concern to clarify it and restate it as well as he can without criticism.

A sample triad conversation went as follows:

Participant 1. (Statement of Concern) "I think we need more materials to work with. In my social studies class I have only one textbook and some of the kids can't read it. Their attitudes are not very good and I get tired of trying to pull them along so that they can pass the achievement test and be ready for the next grade.''

Participant 2. (Perception Check) ''In other words, you think we need multiple texts at a variety of reading levels.''

Participant 1. (Verification and Clarification) ''Yes, and we need some films and overhead projectors to supplement the books.''

Participant 3. (Perception Check) ''I heard you say that we need multiple texts, with supplementary books and audio-visual materials.''

Participant 1. (Restatement of Concern to Be Recorded) ''Yes, let's put it down as follows: We need a variety of text books supported by audio-visual materials, overhead projectors and other supportive materials in order to improve the learning environment in social studies classes.''

As you can see from the above example, the *triad technique* has several advantages.

1. It gives each person an opportunity to be heard.
2. It gives each person the benefit of the feedback from others before he is required to state his concern finally.
3. It gives each person a feeling that his concern is a worthy one and that his colleagues want to help him instead of criticize his efforts.
4. It gives the person an opportunity to evaluate his own statement and restate it as he wants it recorded.

INVOLVEMENT OF PARENTS AND STUDENTS

The principal has made a good beginning in the process of harvesting concerns of faculty members—the first step in a needs assessment. He was now ready to begin involvement of parents, students and the policy makers of the district. He did this only, however, after the faculty was comfortable with the whole idea and the possibility of threat to them had been lessened.

Before going into the community the principal wisely elicited the support of his superintendent or policy group. He needed their *sanction* and support. He also established a reporting system so that they were kept informed and could be called upon to assist as needed.

At the local school level, the involvement of parents was on a selective basis. Not all parents could or would participate. However, those parents who really wished to participate were given the opportunity to do so. The principal began by using his best means of communication with parents. This could have been through the PTSA or parent student groups, but he chose the school bulletin in an effort to provide every member of the community an opportunity to attend a meeting and to influence the processes.

The involvement of students began simultaneously with the involvement of parents so that they could feel equal partnership in the endeavor.

Each of these efforts provided participants with an opportunity for stating a wide variety of concerns. Each group gained an understanding of what was going on and an impression of openness and acceptance within the process.

NOMINATION TECHNIQUES

A system for the selection of representation had to be used to get a workable sized group. During the course of the first meeting with parents, a process of selection of representation was begun. The technique used for this selection was the *nomination technique*. This technique involved the nomination of opinion leaders by the parents, teachers and students—each in separate groups. The nomination technique is similar in many respects to the familiar sociogram; however, in this case it is to identify those persons who are "central" to the opinion norms of the group rather than isolated from it.

The nomination technique involved the listing by each participant of no more than three persons whose opinions he valued in the community, the school, or the student body respectively. By a frequency count the opinion leaders emerged. Often a single individual was listed by as many as 40 or 50 percent of the group, while others were listed only once. The tabulation of nominations was done by the principal, a teacher and one student, with the agreement that data were to be confidential. By listing nominees in rank order, the selection of a group of parents, teachers and students whom others trust was assured.

This was the group, then, that became the steering committee for the needs assessment from that point on and fostered an informal communication with the groups they represented. The steering committee consisted of ten parents, ten teachers and ten students. The tasks for the group were:

1. The evaluation and refinement of areas of concern.
2. The checking of concerns to determine "what is." (Data gathering)
3. The clarifying of values and criteria. (What ought to be)
4. The listing of discrepancies between what is and what ought to be. (the needs)

The steering committee was further broken down into four task forces to accomplish these tasks.

REFINEMENT OF AREAS OF CONCERN

Areas of concern of parents, teachers and students, no matter how well stated, were a hodgepodge of ideas, perceptions and desires, not all of equal worth. They had to be categorized by putting them into useful clusters. Broad categories with subcategories emerged. The broad categories were:

Curriculum: What should be taught?

Methods: How should teaching be conducted?

Materials: What things should be used in the teaching processes?

Out of School Environment: How could the out of school environment be used or improved to support learning?

In School Environment: How could the school learning environment be improved to support learning?

Services: What services were needed by students to support a healthy learning situation?

Parent Support: How could parents be supportive of the school?

School District Support: How could the resources of the central office be used or improved to support good learning?

Student Activities: In what way could student participation be improved to support good learning?

Under each of the categories, concerns were listed comprehensively by rank order. No area of concern was dropped, however, unless it was entirely foreign to the whole effort.

USING THE QUESTIONNAIRE TO CHECK VALIDITY OF CONCERNS

The task force for refining areas of concern wanted to see how valid the list of concerns was. They did this by conducting an *opinion survey*. The categories formed the basis for the compilation of the survey instrument. The instrument asked parents, teachers and students to rate the importance of the expressed concern. It was clearly stated that the school was conducting a needs assessment and wished to know what the most important concerns were. It also was made clear that the items were simple areas of concern and should not be considered as a list of criticisms of the school.

School personnel are very sensitive to criticism, especially from parents, and are reluctant to put themselves into positions where criticism appears to be elicited. This questionnaire (or opinion survey) is not requesting parents to list what is wrong with the school, but instead it asks what the major concerns are. These are a different order of questions than criticism. The purpose of this questionnaire was made clear to all.

A questionnaire was designed to elicit information about how important the respondent considers the issue or concern (See Figure 2-2).

SAMPLE OPINION SURVEY

How important do you consider the following things to your school?

Directions:

Rate each item: 1. Highly important

2. Somewhat important
3. Important, but not as important as other things
4. Not very important
5. Not important at all

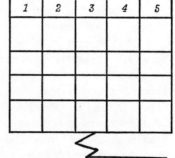

1. Having the most up-to-date teaching materials and equipment

2. Improving school discipline

3. Improving recreational facilities

4. Instituting a career education program

Add any comments you wish on the reverse side of the questionnaire.

Figure 2-2

The tabulation of this opinion survey gave the task force a prioritized list of refined concerns representative of each group: parents, teachers and students. These were the things to gather data about.

CHECKING TO DETERMINE WHAT THINGS ARE LIKE NOW (DATA GATHERING)

The task force for checking the concerns selected those things which were rated most highly to work on. It was not possible to exhaustively study every concern. A realistic cutoff point was established at the six highest rating concerns in each category. Those concerns which were highest on the list were those dealt with.

The degree of sophistication to be applied in data gathering had to be determined. Resources available also had to be considered. Could the school obtain the assistance of a graduate student on a part-time basis or otherwise get staff to help do an adequate job of data gathering? It was decided that the lack of highly technical statistical and sampling capabilities should not be a deterrent to further effort. In every case accuracy would be assured in gathering data, but sophisticated statistical analysis would not be required.

In this community the list of sources of data were as follows:

1. The central office record system
2. The public health department
3. Local school test records
4. Surveys of student participation in school and community
5. Welfare department
6. School attendance records

7. Expenditure rates for teaching staff, materials, school maintenance
8. Follow-up records of students who had gone on to high school
9. Recreational department of the city
10. Boy Scout, Girl Scout, 4-H Club participation records
11. School lunch participation
12. Material selection procedures of the school

The watchword here was accuracy. The task force desired a true picture of what the situation was. Figure 2-3 is an example of the charting procedure used.

RECORDING OF EVIDENCE

Area of Concern	Evidence	Analysis
Reading	Reading survey tests	Degree of reading achievement matched to expectation
Recreational facilities	Survey of recreational facilities	Availability of needed facilities listed
Better discipline	Observation of student behavior and records of disciplinary action	Description of range of behavior compared to expectation

Figure 2-3

The findings by the task force were eventually interpreted into a set of conclusions such as the following:

1. Most students read at or above grade level expectation. Those who fell below grade level read near their expectation when you consider such things as IQ. However, some students who appeared to be at or above average ability fell far below reasonable expectations—about four percent were in this category.
2. Recreational facilities in the school consisted of a gym which was closed after school and on Saturdays. There was one swimming pool open three months in the summer and requiring an admission charge of 35¢. There were no 4-H clubs and only two Boy Scout troops.
3. Discipline was not bad. Only one percent of the children had been known to the police. Noisy children were not considered discipline cases.

Clarifying values. What ought to be: Here the task force looked to the goals for the schools. Every school district has its goals either expressed locally or through state agencies. The goals were a place to begin in considering what ought to be.

The goals addressed such concerns as:

Skills
Attitudes
Knowledge
Citizenship
Personal growth and development
Vocational preparation

The task force revised and redesigned these goals into a set of criteria against which the concerns could be screened. The real test was to validate them. Were they adequate to establish discrepancy between what is and what ought to be? If one area of concern that received a high level of expression on the opinion survey is that of differentiating the curriculum to reflect pluralistic concerns of minority groups represented in the community, this then becomes a valued concern in the community and the goals should include this area of concern. Thus it should be added as a goal.

Listing discrepancies: These are the areas of concern which show the greatest deviation from the goals or values (what ought to be).

In the case of the middle school used in this example, the needs were summarized as:

1. A need for more varied and appropriate instructional materials.
2. A need to provide free recreational opportunities for students after school and on Saturdays.
3. A need for realistic class sizes to permit more individualization.
4. The need for a curriculum reflecting cultural pluralism.
5. A need for cultural minority children to gain identity.
6. A need for a more consistent skill development program, especially for students who were not achieving adequately.
7. A need for more emphasis on career awareness programs for students who were not aware of opportunities which could become available to them.

The above illustration is a simplification of *a community-based needs* assessment model. It presents all of the essential steps in a needs assessment process.

1. Concerns were harvested.
2. Data were gathered to determine "what is."

3. Goals were established to determine "what ought to be."
4. Discrepancies were established between "what is" and "what ought to be."

The community-based model presented here has many advantages.

It is comprehensive. All elements of the community were involved. By this process those who were to be influenced by the process were involved in it, assuring that the concerns were relevant and that the process could result in a broad commitment on the part of all of the community in any plan of action that might result.

There were several elements of risk involved at almost every level of the operation. You will only want to undertake such a process if you are fully prepared to take such risks. Risks include confusion as to who are the designated policy makers of the district. These policy makers are the Superintendent and Board of Education. Will they permit this kind of community influence to be exerted on them? Such a process will surely result in a demand for action. This kind of pressure will be a threat to some policy makers. Along the way certain teachers will worry about their prerogatives and ask why parents and children are permitted to tell professionals what to do. Then, inevitably, resources will be needed to implement improvement programs.

The rewards can be high. By using this process you, as an administrator, will have a set of alternatives which point in a direction and which are well understood by the community. You will have backing from most of the community and from most of the staff for your school improvement program.

The opportunity for creative new approaches will be evident. By this process new insights can be gained as to how schools can develop into creative innovative centers of learning. This process will give a lasting commitment to effort.

Needs assessments can be and are made at all levels of education. Title III of the Elementary and Secondary Education Act required that the State Educational Agency conduct needs assessments in order to qualify for federal funds. These needs assessments formed the basis for setting priorities for the granting of funds to local projects. Most state assessments have been made under the leadership of a steering committee of parents and educators, with occasional representation by students.

District level needs assessments are also conducted from time to time for general or specific needs. Most often large school districts center their needs assessments on building projections and needs. These are usually conducted again by experts, often under the guidance of a citizens' steering committee. Again, the process is the same:

1. What are we concerned about?
2. What is the present situation?

3. What are our values and goals?
4. What are the discrepancies between what is and what ought to be?

The community based model will result in the most valid needs assessment, with the highest degree of commitment by the greatest number of people.

SUMMARY

Everyone makes decisions about what he will do next. If this process is formalized, one has made a needs assessment. There are four steps to a formalized needs assessment process. These are:

1. Identifying areas of concern.
2. Determining what the conditions are (what is).
3. Clarifying values or criteria (what ought to be).
4. Listing the needs (discrepancy between what is and what ought to be).

This chapter presented a case study showing techniques for each of these steps as applied to an exemplary situation.

The first step, identifying areas of concern, is a process for "harvesting" concerns. At this point in a needs assessment, the task is to collect a broad array of concerns. It consists of asking people (parents, teachers and students) what the important things are that schools should achieve. These are then analyzed and refined into a set of concerns which can be agreed upon.

The second step of determining "what is" is more technical. It requires some research. Data sources must be listed, gathered and summarized. After this is done, those conducting the needs assessment are ready to take the next step in the process, agreeing upon what ought to be.

The third step of listing the values or criteria is one which requires agreement upon which things are most important. Here, good statements of goals and objectives are useful. Also, it is useful to look at the original statement of concerns to see which received the highest priority. These then are the things which are most highly valued.

The final step is to list those discrepancies which exist between what is and what should be. These are the needs of the district.

Needs assessment can be formal or informal. The processes can be applied at any level in the school organization. The process usually varies when applied to the local school level, the district level or the state level. Even though the process may differ, it is usually in the extent of participation and research technology applied. The basic steps are always the same.

3

Consensus Techniques for the Selection of Goals and Development Objectives

Why is it that so few people have a clear picture of what is going on in school? Everyone has some idea of what they think schools are doing, and most people have a pretty good idea of what they think schools ought to do. Yet few can tell you what schools *are* doing. If this were true only of the general public, it would be understandable, but it is also true of those persons closest to the schools: Board members, administrators, and teachers. Responsible estimates, backed by research, indicate that there is only about a 25 percent overlap among perceptions commonly held about school programs by the groups which should know the most about their schools. This estimate is shown diagrammatically in Figure 3-1.

PERCEPTION OF WHAT THE SCHOOLS ARE DOING	
	Central Range of Perception
Board of Education Members	
Superintendent of Schools	
Principal of the School	
Classroom Teacher	

▓▓▓ Common Agreement

Figure 3-1

There is little agreement in perception because much of what is stated by the above groups is imprecise and general. There is a high degree of vagueness

43

in expectations of what schools are to accomplish. Few state departments of education and even fewer school districts have tried to define clearly their goals and objectives. The goals and objectives which have been defined carefully are usually piecemeal, applying only to a few subjects or programs, and do not give a holistic picture.

The need, therefore, is for school systems to think more precisely about an adequate, comprehensive set of goals and objectives which will present an understandable set of intentions or commitments. These goals and objectives could be communicated to all groups concerned and be used as outcomes against which to measure general accomplishments of the schools.

GOALS AND OBJECTIVES

These days, we hear much about the terms *goals* and *objectives*, particularly about *behavioral objectives*. Each term is beginning to acquire a set of meanings commonly accepted by the educational community.

In ordinary planning, for example, goals and objectives are terms with separate and distinct meanings. A *goal* identifies a target and is usually descriptive of a long-range program of from one to five years in scope. Goals are established as guides for action, forming the principal basis for developing more precise objectives to follow. On the other hand, *objectives* are specific outcomes anticipated as a result of systematic organized managerial or instructional activities. When objectives meet precise criteria, they become *behavioral objectives*.

Behavioral objectives are precise because they always give the following kinds of information. They tell:

1. Who the intended performer is.
2. What he is to do.
3. Where he is to do it.
4. How well he is to do it.
5. Within what period of time he will accomplish it.

Goals are derived from needs; objectives are means for achieving goals. For example: There is a need for an effective reading program in the district as a whole. The precise need may be determined by looking for discrepancy between what the reading achievement *is* and what we think it *ought* to be.

If data indicate that there is a discrepancy, then a general objective for the system could be to improve the overall level of reading achievement. This may be stated as a district program objective: Within a two-year period, performance will be increased by one year on a reading achievement test administered by the time pupils complete the sixth grade.This program objective gives a great deal of information to the reader about what is expected, of whom and by when.

To achieve this program objective, many behavioral objectives need to be generated at the classroom level. In every case, these behavioral objectives will meet the criteria for such statements as: who, where, what, how, when. Examples of behavioral objectives would be:

> All first grade children who are ready for formal reading at Kelly School will be able to identify the initial sounds produced by the five consonants *d*, *c*, *f*, *h*, *m* through the use of the first primer in the____Series before the middle of the first school year.

> All first grade students who have entered a formal reading program will be able to decode a one-syllable word containing the phonemic elements of *an, ite, ate, or* and *at* through the use of the primer and workbook exercises contained in the____Series at the time of their completion of the workbook.

Behavioral objectives for other levels of work should be equally precise. They serve as a built-in evaluation plan in addition to functioning as an instructional tool by making explicit to the teacher exactly which members of the class have or have not achieved them. The teacher is then in a position to recycle the instruction for those who did not achieve the objective, to indicate next steps for those who did, or to modify the objective if it appears the expectation was too high or too low.

The arrangements for goals and objectives are always hierarchical: Program goals stem from the overall systems goals. The course objectives stem from the program goals and the teacher's instructional behavioral objectives stem from the course goals, as shown in Figure 3-2.

INTERRELATIONSHIP OF GOALS AND OBJECTIVES

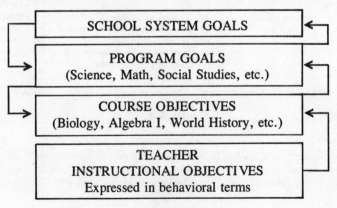

Figure 3-2

No set of goals or objectives is ever independent of other goals and objectives in the hierarchical arrangements. As program goals are generated to reach the system goals, they affect the original statement. Some objectives achieve the goals better than others. Therefore, any plan for generating, stating, or evaluating progress toward reaching goals must provide for an internal monitoring or correction process so that goals and objective statements may themselves be modified as they are used.

In Figure 3-3, the hierarchical statements of goals and objectives, compiled during a cooperative effort of school districts in Oregon and Washington, show the relationship of goals and objectives as stated by the project directors.

<table>
<tr><td rowspan="8">P
L
A
N
N
I
N
G</td><td>System goal: [1]</td><td>The student knows and is able to apply basic scientific and technological processes.</td><td></td></tr>
<tr><td>Program goal:</td><td>The student is able to use the conventional language, instruments, and operations of science.</td><td rowspan="3">To be found in the course goal collections.</td></tr>
<tr><td rowspan="2">Course goal:</td><td rowspan="2">The student is able to classify organisms according to their conventional taxonomic categories from observations, illustrations, or descriptions.</td></tr>
<tr></tr>
<tr><td>Instructional goal:</td><td>The student is able to correctly classify as needleleaf cuttings of the following trees: hemlocks, pines, spruces, firs, larches, cypresses, redwoods, and cedars.</td><td></td></tr>
</table>

<table>
<tr><td rowspan="4">M
E
A
S
U
R
E
M
E
N
T</td><td>Behavioral objective:</td><td>Given cuttings of ten trees, seven of which are needleleaf, the student is able to correctly identify which of the trees are needleleaves.</td><td rowspan="2">Not integral part of Tri-County Project System of Goal-Based Planning.</td></tr>
<tr><td>Performance objective:</td><td>Given cuttings of ten trees, seven of which are needleleaf, the student is able to correctly identify at least six of the seven as belonging to the class of needleleaves.</td></tr>
</table>

Figure 3-3

---

[1] Victor W. Doherty and Walter E. Hathaway. *Introduction to Course Goals for Educational Planning and Evaluation*, K-12, page 20. Copyright 1971, 1973, by the Oregon Local and Intermediate Education School Districts of Clackamas, Multnomah and Washington Counties.

GETTING STARTED

School administrators who wish to implement a plan for designing goals and objectives must prepare a comprehensive plan to do so. Such a plan must include ways of involving those persons most closely affected by the goals. These might include students, parents, teachers, school board members and local community citizens who are concerned about what the schools should teach.

When such a plan is presented to the district, you should expect some questions or objections. Principals will ask, "Who is trying to prescribe the curriculum for all schools?" They may say, "Schools should design their own curriculum to meet the needs of the children who attend."

Teachers may object to a plan because of previous bad experiences with behavioral objectives. Typical remarks would be, "Why is the administration trying to 'ram' more behavioral objectives and accountability down our throats?" They may also feel that someone is trying to make their lives unnecessarily complicated and difficult.

School personnel frequently feel that they have been over such ground before—that this has been tried and failed, or that someone is trying to reinvent the wheel.

These kinds of initial reactions are probably typical. Any school leader who plans to make progress in the direction of having more precise statements of goals and objectives must be prepared to meet them. Simply asking teachers and administrators to begin working on goal statements could encourage organized opposition.

An approach would be to discuss the need for better and clearer statements of goals and objectives and elicit help from teachers and administrators to design methods of achieving some things which they already recognize as needed. For example:

1. The need for clarifying the purposes of education for the students, teachers, parents and the community.
2. The need for better ways to individualize instruction and assure continuous progress for all students.
3. The need for more precise evaluation of the learning that has actually taken place.
4. The need for more effective curriculum and instructional planning, including interdisciplinary planning.
5. The need for better display of the work achieved to answer questions of accountability.

WHO SHOULD PARTICIPATE IN GOAL SETTING?

Another set of concerns centers around the question of involvement. At what level and how much should parents, citizens, school board members and teachers be involved? How can these efforts be coordinated into teamship efforts instead of competing efforts?

A planning group should consider the degree of participation by each group and how they will be involved. A guide for such participation should include the following:

1. *Sanctioning the effort:* The policy-making group, the school board, must understand the need, must approve the plan and must provide resources for the effort.
2. *Setting the systems goals:* Society in general helps to set the overall goals for its schools. Therefore, parents, citizen advisory committees, teachers and students should participate at this level.
3. *Generating the program goals:* Curriculum leaders, subject matter specialists and classroom teachers are best prepared to determine how each program can contribute to reaching a systemwide goal.
4. *Preparing the objectives for each course:* Again, curriculum specialists working together with subject matter specialists and teachers, are best able to coordinate among the grade levels, courses and subjects the various objectives to meet the goals of the programs.
5. *Instructional goals:* Classroom teachers, with the assistance of curriculum leaders, evaluators and subject matter specialists, are best able to write instructional goals and reduce them to behavioral objectives.

By the above distribution of tasks, each group's appropriate role can be clearly defined, and a maximum contribution can be made by each toward the total effort.

The above strategy for involving parents and students in the goal-setting process should begin at the broad goal selection level. This will put them in the position of influencing what the schools should teach.

Some system of representation must be designed to select the participants who will prepare each level of goal statement. At the district goal level, parents and students should be included. If the school system maintains regional advisory groups consisting of parents, interested citizens and student representatives, this is the place to begin. These groups can each nominate one or two of their members to serve on a districtwide committee to work on goals statements. Approximately four parents and four students are needed for each central committee, in addition to the district curriculum design specialists, an evaluation specialist, a principal and three or four classroom teachers (some elementary and some secondary). Each committee should be relatively small in order to promote good working arrangements. The task will be to generate statements of district goals for review and acceptance by other concerned groups. This can be accomplished within a four-week summer workshop. Appropriate payments should be arranged for those participating on the central committee.

The statements of systems goals must reflect the expectations of the community and the larger societies of the state and the nation regarding the kinds of learning that should result from school experience. The best of such goal statements:

a) Are sufficiently general to encompass all outcomes within a relatively few statements.
b) Are expressed in terms of learning, serving the dual needs of the individual and his society.
c) Provide clear direction to program planners in establishing programs and defining curricular goals.
d) Are measurable in terms of broad indicators.

Goal statements are employed principally to inform the citizenry of the broad aims of the school and to elicit their financial and political support, and then as a basis for generating more specific course and subject goals and objectives. These goals should influence the program goals, course goals and the behavioral objectives yet to be developed. The final set of school system goals requires the approval of the school board as the legally constituted policy-making group.

In order to identify the broad areas needing coverage, staff work for the committee should summarize the review of goals from literature, from the state department of education and from previous statements by the district. Broad categories decided upon by the committee might include:

Goals which prepare for social effectiveness.
Goals which prepare for economic efficiency including career education.
Goals which promote the American way of life.
Goals which prepare for participation in government.
Goals which promote an understanding of our changing world.

The committee's role is to generate the goal statements and to validate them. Special techniques are needed to achieve consensus of the committee itself and then to achieve validation. The suggested techniques, similar in nature, will be discussed separately.

THE CONSENSUS TECHNIQUE

This technique is very effective in helping groups reach agreement by providing a means of clarifying intent, making necessary modifications of ideas, and finally producing statements which have few ambiguities and are therefore understandable by others. It also has a built-in prioritizing element.

The technique is a modification of the Delphi technique, which will be fully presented in a later chapter.

The rules of the process are simple.

1. The group must agree upon the criteria for judging each contribution.
2. Each contribution (in this case, a proposed goal statement) is placed in a pool.
3. Each contribution is presented to the group by a member other than the person who wrote it.
4. The presenter reads the contribution made by another, evaluates it according to the criteria and classifies it as meeting a *critical* need, meeting an *important* need or being *helpful* in meeting a need.
5. After the presentation, each member around the table is given an opportunity to react to the original classification. He may ask for clarification, agree or disagree with the classification, but he must always give his reasons for agreeing or disagreeing.
6. The group reaches consensus as to where the contribution should be classified, and it is left tentatively in that category for future consideration.

The technique has the following advantages:

It requires group members to write each statement as carefully as possible because they know it will be presented by another person.

It serves as a perception check; that is, do people understand it? Does it trigger other ideas?

It serves as positive, encouraging feedback. All contributions are classified by a positive term (*critical, important* or *helpful*). There are no negative categories.

It elicits thought and discussion on the part of all members of the group. Each person must respond and give a reason for his response.

It serves as a self-correction device. In subsequent rounds, as final selections are made, the statements become more precise and understandable.

It promotes group solidarity for the reason that each contribution becomes group property as it is eventually modified and corrected in subsequent rounds of discussion. In addition, group members acquire a helping attitude toward other members in the group.

The final product is mutually acceptable and can be supported by each member of the group.

The author has had experience in generating goals of this kind using the consensus technique. The following account shows how the technique works to reduce a collection of vague ideas into a set of precise goal statements.

The group leader, in this case a professional educator, opened the discussion with the task to be performed. Large charts listing statements to which the group could refer were displayed around the room.

Chart No. 1 set forth the objective of the group stated as:

Our Objective

1. To prepare a set of school district instructional goals which meet the established criteria and have them ready for validation by the end of the four-week period

---

Chart No. 2 listed criteria for a good goal.

Criteria for General Goals

1. Sufficiently general to encompass all outcomes within a relatively few statements
2. Expressed in terms of learning, serving the dual needs of the individual and society
3. Provide clear direction to program planners in establishing programs and defining curricular objectives
4. Measurable in terms of broad indicators

Chart No. 3 suggested the categories for which goals were to be prepared.

Goal Categories

1. Intellectual development
2. Physical and mental health
3. Appreciation of fellow men
4. Social effectiveness
5. Economic efficiency
6. Promotion of the American way of life
7. Participation in government
8. Understanding of our changing world

The group began by discussing the objective, the criteria and the categories of goals. More of the discussion centered around the categories in Chart No. 3.

Why these?
What else should be included?
Shouldn't we include the basic skills as a goal?
Where would family life education come in?

These were all good discussion questions and showed that the group was interested, had good concerns and was willing to participate.

The group decided to work within the suggested categories but to add items that they thought were important, even though they didn't see immediately where they might fit.

One way to begin could be to write down the important items and fit them into categories, creating new categories, if necessary. Another way could be to formally analyze each category, listing subtopics to be included into each. The decision in this case was made to do the former, that is, to start by contributing items that members felt were important regardless of whether or not they fit into predetermined categories.

This was a good decision from many standpoints. It released the group from any hard and fast restrictions. It provided for the modification of categories or the creation of new categories as needed. It freed members to work with their major concerns. In this way, they could gain experience and provide for new insights later. Eventually, a systematic analysis of the areas covered would have to be made. This could be done better after more input was on the table.

Each member was instructed to use the next hour to generate two to five statements which expressed a concern that he had regarding what schools should teach. The statements could fit into any category or could be outside the listed ones.

Let's follow through with five statements to see how the flow went in this case and might be expected to go in other instances.

Round 1. Contributions to the Collection.
Statement 1. *The schools should teach every child to read well.*
Statement 2. *The schools should teach children to think for themselves and form their own judgments.*
Statement 3. *All children should be employable upon graduation from high school.*
Statement 4. *Schools should teach patriotism.*
Statement 5. *The schools should teach children to be respectful of parents, government officials, etc.*

Round 2. Presentation and Classification.

In round two, it is important that the person who presents the contribution to the group be someone other than the originator. This serves as a perception check on whether the item can be interpreted by another. The presenter must classify the item as *helpful*, *important* or *critical*, and give his reasons.

Statement 1. *The schools should teach every child to read well.*

Presenter: "I believe this is a critical need, so I would classify it as *critical*. My reason is that no person in modern society can be intellectually developed or economically efficient if he can't read well."

Respondent 1. "I agree with the classification of *critical*, but I'd like to add spelling, writing and arithmetic to this list. I believe that what was said about reading is equally important for these other subjects."

Respondent 2. "This was the item I wrote, and I would accept these other subjects in addition to reading."

Respondent 3. "I agree and have nothing to add."

And so it went through the group.

Consensus was reached that the goals should include the skills of reading, writing, spelling and mathematics and be categorized as meeting a *critical* need.

Statement 2. *The schools should teach children to think for themselves and form their own judgments.*

Presenter: "This is very important, but the statement is highly general. I think we should add to it so that students would be taught 'how' to think, not just to think. I would classify it as *helpful* because I'm not sure that thinking without learning how to think is critical."

Respondent 1. "I believe the person who wrote this had the right idea. If we added something to it about problem identification and problem solution processes, I'd move it up to *critical*."

Respondent 2. "I think it is too general. I'd leave it where it is."

Respondent 3. "I think we should compromise and put this in the *important* pile, then clean it up later."

Consensus was reached to classify the statement as *important* and to work it over later.

Statement 3. *All children should be employable upon graduation from high school.*

Presenter: "I believe most students should be employable, but this statement doesn't have any room for exceptions. How about housewives? Are they employable? Also, employable at what—ditchdigging? I would classify it as *helpful* but not *important* or *critical* at this time."

Respondent 1. "I think it is *critical* that everyone should be employable. Don't we hear a lot about women's lib? Women should be employable, too. I want it classified at least in the *important* category."

Respondent 2. "I can only accept the statement if it is changed to career education. If it is changed to career education, being a housewife could qualify and so could going to college to prepare for a profession. If it were career education, I'd move it to *critical*."

Respondent 3. "I wrote it and really meant career education. I am willing to substitute 'career education' for 'employable.' "

Consensus. The statement should be modified to include career education and should be classified as *critical*.

Statement 4. *Schools should teach patriotism.*

Presenter: "This statement is *helpful* because it focuses attention upon one of the important things that society expects its schools to do, teach patriotism. To be *important* or *critical*, the statement should be more specific. Patriotism is too general a term."

Respondent 1. "I agree that substituting something like 'understand the American way of life' or 'participation in government' would be a better statement."

Respondent 2. "Let's move it to *important* and substitute 'preparation for participating effectively in the American way of life.' "

Respondent 3. "I don't think we have it yet. Who is to say what patriotism is or what the American way of life is? Let's change it to include preparation for responsible participation in government."

Conclusion: Classify it as *important* but describe more fully what is meant by patriotism.

Statement 5. *The schools should teach children to be respectful of parents, government officials, etc.*

Presenter: "We are again into the area of character building, attitudes and values. I think we will have to work very hard on this statement to make it say what we really mean. I'd classify it as *important* for now and work it over later."

Respondent 1. "I agree, let's leave it as *important* and work it over later."

Consensus: Classify it as *important* and work it over later.

The preceding narrative illustrates how the modified Delphi or Consensus technique works to generate ideas. It also helps in checking the ideas for clarity to prepare the way for refinement of a set of goal statements that will be both understood and accepted by a broad group of people.

The technique has paved the way for intensive work by committees of one or two to revise, rewrite and edit statements into the intermediate form for further discussion and final acceptance as goals. This can all occur during the formal workshop.

VALIDATION

You will recall that the task required validation. The process of validation is very important. To validate anything is to determine that it does what it says it is going to do. In the case of goals, they will do what they say they are going to do if they meet two conditions.

1. They must communicate to the reader what is meant in the social context.
2. They must be useful to the educational group in generating program goals, course objectives and finally behavioral objects.

The first condition can be achieved by submitting the tentative goals to reference groups for their reaction. The same techniques for gaining consensus can be used by the reference group as by the writing group. However, in this case, the goals will be broken down into individual statements which the reference group can analyze and then classify in the same manner as *critical*, *important* and *helpful*. Ideas and suggestions can be noted, and the goals can be prioritized according to the degree of importance suggested by the various reference groups.

The reference groups are mainly parent groups and professional educational groups selected because of their general interest in education and their degree of acceptance by the community as trusted opinion makers. It is suggested that school advisory committees which are formed for this purpose or which already exist should be used—not groups which already exist for a politically-based set of purposes. Politically-oriented groups or associations tend to have their own criteria and sets of values. They use their groups to foster political action or bring pressure to bear on schools and government agencies and, therefore, would be ineffective. The reference groups should be parent-school councils or advisory committees whose purpose is to assist the schools in doing a better job. Each individual in the group should be responsible only to himself (not a politically motivated group) for his actions and recommendations.

Educators validate the goals by reviewing them and, in the end, by using them. All goal collections are first released for critique with a limited circulation to teachers and curriculum specialists. After one revision is made, based upon feedback from users, a first edition should be issued.

An important step in this procedure is formation of review and revision committees for the goals. The purpose is to assure an unbiased process for authenticating the final collection of goals.

GOALS INTO OBJECTIVES

Essentially, the same process of generating goals and supporting objectives should be followed. As the goals become objectives, they become ever more precise. The job also becomes increasingly a professional responsibility. The community in general participates in setting the overall purposes (goals) for the school. Then professional educators determine how these goals should be reached by preparing the objectives, and are accountable to the public for how they are reached.

Also, the objectives must become more technically precise. As they become behavioral in nature, they require careful review by trained specialists who assist the teachers to perfect them.

Use of standard sources:

There are an increasing number of taxonomies of educational goal statements. In an effort to implement PPBS programs, groups are beginning to compile their own collections of goals and objectives. One of the most thorough and carefully validated sets was that prepared by a consortium of school districts in Oregon and Washington.[2] Such resources are recommended for use by local educational committees who are faced with the task of preparing objectives. The task then becomes a selection process rather than a writing process.

Also, goals and objectives become more numerous at the subject or course level. The use of collections serves as a resource giving teachers the opportunity to select the particular goals and objectives needed for their classes.

When a school system has spent a year or two in the preparation of carefully stated goals, it is equipped for both great educational improvement and growing public confidence. It has also laid the groundwork for more sophisticated entry into careful planning and evaluation. Knowing what these represent, members of the school system can now program a method of achieving their goals, in addition to establishing a procedure for learning how well they are doing.

SUMMARY

The terms "goals" and "objectives" are beginning to acquire a set of

---

[2]Tri County Goal Development Project of Clackamas, Multnomah and Washington Counties. Commercial-Educational Distributing Services, P.O. Box 8723, Portland, Oregon 97208. Copyright 1971, 1973. Disseminated by Northwest Regional Educational Laboratory, 710 S. W. Second Avenue, Portland, Oregon 97204.

meanings commonly accepted by the educational community. Goals identify a target or state a broad intention and form the basis for developing a more precise set of objectives. Objectives are specific outcomes and are ways of meeting the broader goals. When objectives contain specific kinds of information they become behavioral objectives. To be so classified, they must be stated in such a way as to tell: (a) who the intended performer is, (b) what he is to do, (c) where he is to do it, (d) how well he will do it, and (e) within what period of time he will accomplish it.

Goals and objectives are hierarchical; that is, one flows from another. The hierarchy is illustrated in Figure 3-2 of this chapter and includes the categories of (1) School System Goals, (2) Program Goals, (3) Course Objectives, and (4) Instructional Objectives, expressed in behavioral terms.

Many people at several levels should participate in the preparation of goals and objectives. The effort needs the approval of the policy-making group and their financial support. The public in general, particularly the parents and students, should help select the overall district goals. This is because schools should serve the public societal needs and be able to explain to the public how they are going about meeting these needs. Determining the objectives of how these broad needs are met is the job of professional educators. The program goals, the course goals and the teaching objectives are better determined by teachers, curriculum specialists and evaluation specialists.

The criteria for good districtwide goals statements include answers to the following questions:

a. Are they sufficiently general to encompass all outcomes within a relatively few statements?
b. Are they expressed in terms of learning, serving the dual needs of the individual and society?
c. Do they provide clear direction to program planners for establishing program goals and instructional objectives?
d. Are they measurable by broad indicators?

School personnel would be well advised to use standard sources for selection of the courses and instructional objectives. The generation of the original statements is time consuming and extremely costly. The use of well stated and validated standard taxonomies cuts much of this time and effort and puts the process at the *selection* level rather than at the preparation level. After all, the selection is more important than who stated them in the first place. The local school districts still have control over what is included, and that is the important thing.

The generation of goals and objectives for a school district must be an organized long-time process. There have been too many efforts which are piecemeal and ineffective. It can be worth the effort and in fact may be one of the most important things a district can do. A good program of goal development and objectives selection lays the groundwork for many decisions at every level of the school district. It will clearly indicate to both the public and professional personnel where the district is headed, how it intends to get there and how they will know when they have arrived.

4

How to Use the Flow Chart
as a Planning Technique

No one deliberately plans for failure, but the number of educational innovations which are unsuccessful raises the question of subconscious intent. It is quite possible that we as teachers and administrators have built failure into our projects by inadequate planning.

You only need to visit innovative projects two or three years after they are first reported in educational literature, to be impressed with their short lives. Typical responses are: "Oh, that project was very good but the funding stopped" or "It was a good idea but it just didn't work. There were too many problems to overcome."

In almost every case the original concept of the project was good. It was usually designed to do better something that needed to be done. It most likely met with initial enthusiasm and support, but could not be maintained on enthusiasm alone.

Failure usually results when the staff members who implement a project not only must adjust to their new roles and responsibilities, but also are required to cope with unforeseen problems. Any group, regardless of its dedication and skill, solves only a limited number of problems in a given amount of time. The success of an innovation is probably related directly to the number of potential problems that are identified and solved prior to implementation. Therefore, anyone preparing to adopt a new program must consider the planning procedures to be used in designing and implementing a model of the flow of decisions, events and tasks to assure maintenance and self-correction of the project as it proceeds.

One of the most complicated projects ever attempted has been the space program and moon probe. To accomplish this task, NASA had to develop planning procedures capable of handling extremely complex problems. The same kind of planning procedure can be adapted to serve as a model for the planning and implementation of school programs.

The system used by NASA includes many techniques. When put together these become a *systems approach* to planning. The set of technology associated with a systems approach includes many terms which are vaguely familiar to most of us. These include Goal Setting, PERTing, Flow Charting and the Critical Path Method.

It is not the purpose of this chapter to develop a complete discussion of the design of an effective system including systems theory, systems technology, systems techniques and products. Rather, a technique which is central to the whole idea of systematic planning will be presented. This technique is *flow charting*.

Flow charting is a process for describing a procedure with the use of a diagram rather than words. It is useful in many ways and is necessary to the very technical processes of PERT and Critical Path Analysis.

PERT stands for *Program Evaluation Review Technique*. It was developed by the U. S. Navy Special Projects Office to help speed up the space program.

The Critical Path Method was designed jointly by DuPont and Sperry Rand Corporation and is similar to PERT in that both systems help planners and evaluators visualize the plan, assess costs for each step of progress and make decisions about the best sequence of events, *the critical path*, to be followed. Flow Charting is the method of displaying this critical path.

Flow Charting employs geometric figures and lines, instead of narration, to describe job procedures, work flow and information processing routine.

FLOW CHARTING TECHNIQUES

Broken down into its simplest form, a flow chart is a straight line between a beginning point to an end product showing the major intervening events and decisions. Figure 4-1 is an example of a problem-solving sequence of events in a systematic decision process.

This is a very simple straight sequence of major events for problem solving.

The problem-solving model is used here because it is universal. Its systematic steps should always be considered when making a flow chart. If the planner is going to deviate from this model, he should do it because of reasons, not because he has forgotten an important consideration in the sequence.

You will notice that the events in this example are listed in rectangles □ except for Event 5, which is a diamond ◇ for a decision point. These designa-

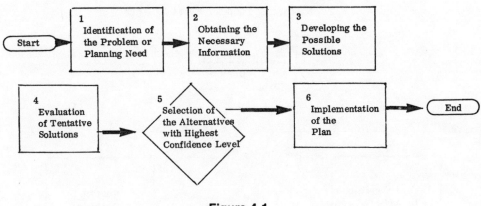

Figure 4-1

tions are consistent with the American Standard flow charting symbols. By using these symbols, the reader is immediately alerted to important points in the flow that indicate the beginning or ending of the flow ⬭ ; the designation of a process or event □ and the major decision points in the total process ◇.

SUPPORTING LOOPS

Addition of loops supporting a particular event is the next step. Any one of the major events in the flow can be supported by a subset of activities. These are shown as individual flow loops to add detailed clarity to what occurs before one event is complete. Let's take Event 1 (Figure 4-2), the identification of the problem or planning need, and break it down into a supporting loop of activities.

PROCESS ROSTER OF ACTIVITIES

This loop of activities specifies that the problem be analyzed by:

1A. Listing the conditions to be affected; that is, the effect of the problem on the school system or learner and the rationale for selecting it as a priority.
1B. Listing the alternative outcomes, i.e., listing all the possible things that could be achieved in terms of outcomes which will alleviate or solve the problem.
1C. Making a decision as to which of the potential outcomes will be sought.

Supporting Loop for Event 1

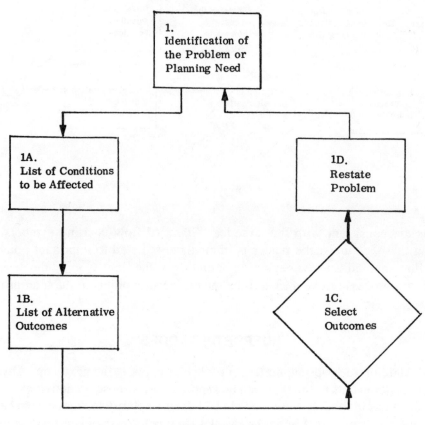

Figure 4-2

1D. Restating the problem supported by the specific outcomes expected, after the decision is made.

This sequence of activities assures careful consideration of the elements which go into a well-stated problem, taking the problem from a set of somewhat vague ideas to an explicit statement. The statement will be carefully analyzed and the basis for rational decisions can be documented.

PREPARING A PROCESS ROSTER

Before the supporting loop could be completed for Event 1, *Identification of the Problem or Need*, a job roster or list of essential activities is a desirable but nonmandatory step. If the flow charter has all job processes pertaining to a particular job firmly in mind, he may elect to omit developing a roster of the processes involved. On the other hand, if he is at all unclear as to the sequence of processes or the nature of the decisions which need to be included in his flow chart, he should develop a roster.

Let us apply this model to two problems which a school might meet. One is a program problem and the other is needed planning.

PROGRAM PROBLEM

Valley Town had always had several Chicano children in its schools. These children were from migrant families and stayed only during harvest time. Consequently, their lack of achievement and disassociation with the school was hardly evident. However, things were changing. The families were taking up permanent residences in the town. The conditions regarding the lack of achievement and disinterest in school could no longer be swept under the rug.

The general problem to be addressed was: How can Valley Town improve the education of Chicano children in the elementary grades?

Now let's apply the first process loop to this general problem.

The supporting loop for process 1, Identification of the Problem, designates four processes. A roster of these processes would look like the following.

1A. *List conditions to be affected.*

Condition 1. Children do not speak English well.

Condition 2. Children do not learn to read well.

Condition 3. Children do not attend school regularly and show a disinterest in the school activities.

Condition 4. Parents complain that their children do not have equal opportunity with the Anglo children.

1B. *List specific outcomes desired.*

Possible Outcome 1. Children will feel that their culture is respected at school.

Possible Outcome 2. Children will read things that interest them.

Possible Outcome 3. Children will show more interest in the school and attend regularly.

Possible Outcome 4. Parents will communicate with the schools about their feelings for the school.

Possible Outcome 5. Children will improve their Spanish as well as English.

Possible Outcome 6. Children will improve their reading skills.

Possible Outcome 7. Anglo and Chicano children will develop mutual respect.

1C. *Select Specific Outcomes* ◇ *Decision.*

The decision would be to attempt to achieve as many of the possible outcomes as reasonable.

1D. *Write the problem supported by outcomes.*

Valley Town will improve the educational program for Chicano children in order that they may:
1. Feel pride in their culture
2. Improve their reading and speaking
3. Show more interest in school
4. Have the support of their parents

This example traced a program through the first major event and support loop, the *Identification of the Problem* or *Planning Need.*

The second example is a Planning Need rather than a Problem.

1A. The conditions to be affected are:
1. Teachers in Valley Town use few audiovisual materials.
2. Each school is attempting to buy its own audiovisual equipment, which often breaks down and is out of service.
3. Teachers order films from rental centers individually.
4. Films often arrive and are used by one teacher, while others in the school system may need them.
5. There is no audiovisual specialist to consult with teachers about use of materials.

1B. Listing alternative (possible) outcomes desired.
1. Teachers will plan well for the use of the best teaching materials.
2. Coordinated use of materials will be provided.
3. Necessary equipment will be available on interschool loan.
4. Teachers will have necessary assistance in planning for and selecting audiovisual materials.

1C. Making a decision as to which of the potential outcomes will be sought.

All of the outcomes may be considered desirable. If so, each one would be put into the final problem statement.

1D. Restating the problem.

The problem then was to improve audiovisual service to teachers in Valley Town to assure the wise and coordinated use of audiovisual materials, supported by consultant service of a specialist and well-maintained and available equipment.

The flow charter will want continually to raise two questions:

Process Roster

(List of Activities and Decisions)

2. Obtaining the necessary information

Process Identification	Processes	Decisions
A.	Collect data	
B.	Do literature search	
C.	Conduct interviews and review test data	
D.	Select pertinent information to be used	◇

3. Developing possible solution

A.	List alternative solutions	
B.	List conditions which effect each solution	
C.	Select tentative solution	◇

4. Evaluation of tentative solution

A.	List conditions which favor the solution	
B.	List conditions which disfavor the solution	
C.	Select ways of overcoming the unfavorable conditions to be considered	◇
D.	Prepare the materials for review	

5. Decision (Selection of the alternative with the greatest potential)

A.	Review the data	
B.	Assemble the decision group	
C.	Present the favorable and unfavorable conditions for each potential solution	
D.	Recommend the alternative with the greatest potential	
E.	Decision by the decision group	◇

6. Implementation of the Plan

A.	Prepare job description	
B.	Select the staff	
C.	Orient and train the staff	
D.	Prepare time lines	
E.	Prepare decision matrix	
F.	Get final approval (sanction from Policy Group)	◇
G.	Begin work	

Figure 4-3

1. What job process or decision, if any, must precede the process or decision point under consideration?
2. What job process or decision, if any, must immediately follow the process or decision point under consideration?

The general model given in Figure 4-1 is too gross to assure a sequential work flow. A process roster for Event 1 was suggested for each of two major problems in Valley Town.

Process rosters for Events 2 through 6 are shown in outline form in Figure 4-3.

Put all together, the flow chart is much more detailed than before. Each major event is now supported by a loop of events which must be accomplished before moving on. The skeleton of this flow chart appears in Figure 4-4.

A SKELETAL FLOW CHART WITH SUPPORTING LOOPS

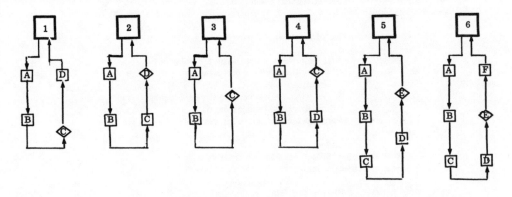

Figure 4-4

The main line or path of events is shown by the top line.

The activities which must be performed to achieve the major events are shown in the loops under each task.

ADDING DETAIL TO FLOW CHARTS

In order to be a meaningful flow chart, each box must be filled with the appropriate event or task, as the case may be. The flow chart must have identified each major event in proper sequence and the supporting loop of activities which are necessary to complete the event. The level of detail will depend upon the thoroughness of the planning. Theoretically, every activity could be broken down into *tasks* and every task into subtasks, etc. If careful cost analysis is to be made, then the more detailed the flow chart is the more accurate the cost projection becomes. An example is Figure 4-5.

LEVELS OF ACTIVITIES

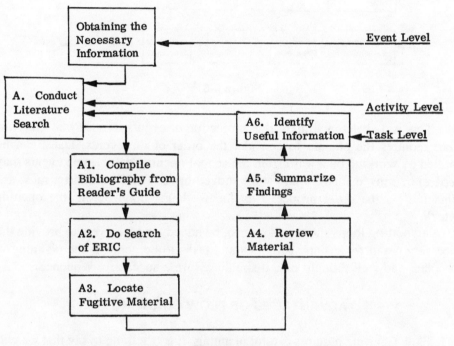

Figure 4-5

With this amount of detail the flow chart becomes ever more accurate and useful in anticipation of costs, personnel, materials, etc. The guesswork is minimized in such estimates.

The use of flow charting supported by process rosters permitted Valley Town to alleviate (not solve) two pressing problems. One was a *program problem* concerning an influx of Chicano children, as the school needed a more effective program for them. The other problem was a *planning need* concerning the establishment of a system of audiovisual service.

The problem-solving model was effective for these problems. Another model might be more effective for another situation. Take a major happening, the opening of a new school.

Major events in this process shown in a straight line projection would include those shown in Figure 4-6.

STRAIGHT LINE PROJECTION OF EVENTS

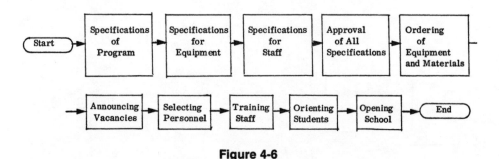

Figure 4-6

This is a skeleton straight-line projection of events. Notice that this flow chart requires the planner to consider the order of the events. Dates can be applied by working backward from the school opening date. Some events may need to be moved forward and some moved back. The flow charter must ask himself, "Is the order proper? Can the work get done before the opening date?"

Supporting loops should, of course, be added for each event to provide the necessary detail for events, activities and tasks to be done. If the planning is complete and well thought out, it should assure a successful sequence.

ADVANTAGES OF FLOW CHARTING

1. Flow Charting requires careful planning. It is one thing to say that we will conduct a study or that we will prepare a new course of study, but it is another thing to be required to show the detailed steps which will be followed in doing so. Flow Charting requires the planner to be specific, not general, in his plans.
2. Flow Charting requires sequential ordination of events. A flow chart requires the planner to put things in proper order. It also requires those who implement the plan to complete one event before starting another. In other words, a worker simply cannot get ahead of himself. He cannot do the literature search until the problem has been carefully stated and supported, etc.
3. Flow Charting clearly identifies decision points. The planner who uses Flow Charting is required to look carefully for events in the process which require decisions (choices). Any management plan must identify points in processes that need approval and sanction to proceed. Sanction from the policy group (the superintendent or Board) is very important to any development. It gives assurance of support to the worker and it provides the

policy group an opportunity to exercise their leadership and assume their share of accountability. Flow Charting identifies those points beforehand so that all understand at what point this approval is needed.

4. Flow Charting provides a clear display of a plan from beginning to end. A well-built flow chart should provide necessary assurances to those who must make decisions that good planning has been done. The display of events in a flow chart will also trigger suggestions and make omissions apparent for correction.

5. Flow Charting provides a device for monitoring progress. Another dimension of a flow chart is the timeline. Across the top of the chart the time sequence should be included. This predicts the dates of completion of each event. As the events are completed they can be so designated on the chart.

6. Flow Charting can lead to accurate cost projection. As pointed out before, the more detailed a flow chart becomes the better the cost estimate becomes. The planner is not caught in the bind of heavy unanticipated expenses or costly delays by simply having overlooked some piece of work which needed to be done.

SIMULTANEOUS ACTIVITIES

It was pointed out earlier that Flow Charting requires ordination; that is, what comes first, what comes second, etc. In some cases several activities can be undertaken simultaneously, leading to the completion of an event. These activities can be shown by breaking the flow and branching the activities, and then bringing them all back into sequence. For example, if a piece of material

SIMULTANEOUS ACTIVITIES

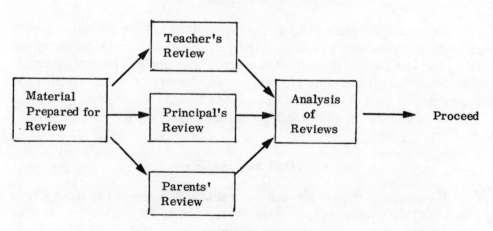

Figure 4-7

must be submitted to several groups for review before the project can proceed, it would be foolish not to do this simultaneously, as shown in Figure 4-7.

THE CLOSED LOOP

When a certain process is intended to be repeated several times, the closed loop is an appropriate flow charting technique. The main characteristic of a closed loop is that it is a self-corrective process. It feeds information back into its own objectives. Generally speaking, the teaching event will be repeated several times. Each time it should get better. As evaluation occurs, objectives are clarified and the process is improved. This closed loop is shown in Figure 4-8.

CLOSED LOOP

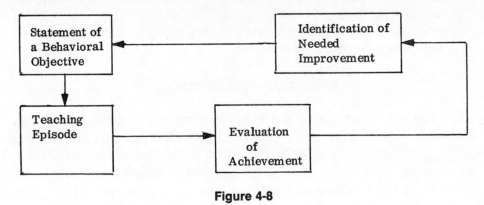

Figure 4-8

BRANCHING

Some complex plans call for alternative future actions that might lead to entirely different courses of action. These can be shown by branching of the flow chart into the two or more alternatives. For example, a plan might anticipate either designing an entirely new course of study or simply revising the present course, or a third alternative would be to leave the present course as is. This branching can be shown in a flow chart (Figure 4-9).

COST ESTIMATES

The resources needed for each event should be estimated as accurately as possible. This is done by preparing backup sheets for each event, task or subtask, depending upon the level of detail used in the plan. The backup sheets

BRANCHING

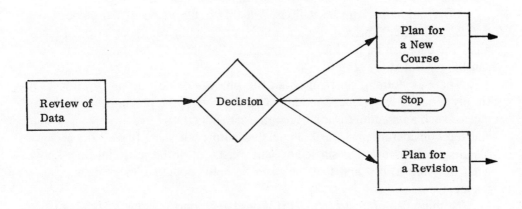

Figure 4-9

should contain estimates of personnel by days per task, consultants (if any), supplies and materials, equipment, travel (if any), and other anticipated costs.

For example, obtaining the necessary information may require a literature search, review of lists, interviewing and other learner data, copyright/patent search and selection of pertinent information. An estimate would include the man-days required for various personnel, such as:

1. Director of the project—10 person days for planning and supervision
2. Research assistant—20 person days for locating material
3. Clerical assistance—30 person days
4. A consultant—one day to advise on data location and one day to assist in the review of data collected

Equipment: A cassette recorder is needed to record interviews: (A decision must be made whether to rent or purchase a recorder). Also, office equipment and typewriters are needed.

Travel: Mileage must be provided for interviewers.

Supplies: Paper and other incidental supplies.

Printing: A final report should be duplicated in X number of copies at an estimate of X number of total pages.

Facilities: Three office spaces are needed.

So it goes. This is very detailed planning for each event or task. A compilation of such backup sheets will reveal the number of person days needed for the project, together with a total budget. In other words, the budget for the project, including the staffing plan, is a result of the needs of each planning task rather than some gross estimate for the total project.

Cost estimating can be tedious, but this is the name of the game if the critical path of cost-effective plan is to be chosen. In very sophisticated planning, the data can be fed into a computer and alternative combinations of data can be generated for review.

There is nothing magical about the process of costing-out a project. It simply requires experienced judgment on the part of the planners. The advantage of such a procedure is that it requires consideration of each sequential step and the consideration of costs associated with each step. If well done, such planning will assure that sufficient staff exists to do the job, that they know what they are to do, and that they can be held accountable for their performance.

Nothing can protect a project if it has been poorly planned. If unrealistically high costs have been put into the plan, it will not be cost effective. If costs have been projected at a figure that is too low, then the job cannot be accomplished. In its simplest form, planning is a system of systematic estimation. The flow charting process is supposed to assure that the best and most reasonable estimates have been made.

SUMMARY

Many good projects have failed because of lack of careful planning. One of the most persistent needs for those who are planning a new venture is to use a consistent and accurate technique for deciding step by step what it will take to get from "where I am" to "where I want to go."

Various names are given to the process of planning recommended in this chapter. PERT (Program Evaluation Review Technique) and its related Critical Path Analysis are the processes adopted by the Department of Defense to assure good planning. When these processes are reduced to a diagrammatical display, the result is a flow chart from the beginning (start) to the (end). All of the intervening events, activities and tasks can be shown in the amount of detail necessary to assure sequential development of the project.

When the flow charting has been done carefully, the human and material resources can be calculated precisely. If the process is carefully done, success usually is assured, barring adverse affective circumstances or unknown interference with the process.

In its simplest form, flow charting is a straight line, displaying the major events from the beginning to the end result (See Fig. 4-1). Events are shown in boxes. A rectangle □ stands for a piece of work to be done. A diamond ◇ represents a major decision point in the flow. Each event can be broken down into all of the supporting activities showing the decision points within this supporting loop (see Fig. 4-2).

Before a flow chart can be done, it is important to prepare a process roster. This is a list of the activities and decision points under each of the major events for the entire flow. Flow charting then is employed to display the relationships of these activities to the general flow of work.

Detail to the task level and subtask level can be added to the extent needed by the project. The more the detail the more precise becomes the plan, and it gives a better basis for estimating personnel needs (person days), time, space, resources and other needs.

Flow charting has the following advantages.

1. It requires careful planning.
2. It requires sequential ordination of events.
3. It clearly identifies decision points.
4. It provides a clear display of the plan from beginning to end.
5. It provides a device for monitoring progress.
6. It can lead to accurate cost projection.

Variations of flow charting can accommodate simultaneous activities (see Fig. 4-7) and branching activities (see Fig. 4-9). Also, a closed loop diagram can be helpful in illustrating a process which is cyclical and often repeated (see Fig. 4-8).

As pointed out in the chapter, nothing can protect a poorly conceived project from failure and sometimes even the best planned projects do not succeed. Flow charting, however, requires the level of planning which can make the difference between success and failure for a well-conceived project.

5

Understanding Key Factors in PPBS— Planning, Programming, Budgeting Systems

There is growing pressure on educators to expend scarce educational resources more effectively and efficiently, and to account for the use of these resources with greater fidelity. The public wants to know about efficiency because it indicates lack of waste of resources. They want to know about effectiveness because it indicates achievement of goals. The two go hand in hand. We really cannot achieve one without the other, for what would be the use of an economical educational system which didn't do the job; and on the other hand, what would be the use of having a good educational system which was wasteful and which nobody could afford?

The pressures on school leaders to answer the questions about efficiency and effectiveness are finding focus nationwide through failed school district tax levies and state legislative mandates for performance planning and evaluation of education. As a result, educators at every level of the educational endeavor are reaching for ways to define their goals more clearly, to attain the goals in an efficient way and to evaluate the attainment of goals so that they can know how well they are doing.

The system which has most relevance to this whole task is the Planning, Programming, Budgeting System (PPBS). The system itself, like so many other systems, has been adapted for educational use from another field of endeavor. It was developed as a systems approach to planning and budgeting for the Defense Department of the United States government. It was a popular innovation and received President Lyndon Johnson's sanction as the system to be used in all government agencies for planning and cost projections.

Attempts to apply it to state and local public agencies were immediate. Its popularity is directly related to its potential for clarifying the planning and budgeting procedures of public agencies and the confidence the public holds for systematic analysis of the use of resources.

Essentially, PPBS involves the development and orderly presentation of relevant information pertaining to the costs and benefits of major alternative courses of action. PPBS does not examine such problems as budget implementation, manpower selection, or cost control. These and other such aspects should be considered as complementary to PPBS rather than a direct part of it.

The advantages of the system are: (1) PPBS focuses on identifying goals and objectives. (2) Future year implications are explicitly considered. (3) All costs of alternatives are considered, including capital, non-capital and associated (fixed) support costs. (4) It provides top level administrators with a review of major cost and benefit tradeoffs among alternatives.

The disadvantages of the system are: (1) PPBS has to date not helped much in deciding on ultimate goals or even in deciding between alternative goals. (2) PPBS requires experienced analytical personnel to implement and monitor it. (3) PPBS requires extensive information on costs, planning factors and evaluation of benefits. (4) In order to receive maximum benefit from the system, an entire school organization must become PPBS oriented.

PPBS is a comprehensive system requiring sequential and coordinated efforts on the part of the planners. The sophisticated Western New York PPBS Model categorizes these into four major steps diagrammatically displayed (Figure 5-1).

1. PLANNING
   - School staff and students and community residents are surveyed regularly to collect data for educational decision making.
   - Data collected are analyzed and summarized into statements of the community's educational needs.
   - Priorities of identified needs are established.
   - Statements of district goals and objectives are generated for all areas of educational need.
2. PROGRAMMING
   - A Program Structure allowing for the organizational examination of objectives and activities is developed by the district.
   - Specific objectives are generated, consistent with district goals and objectives, at all levels of the Program Structure.
   - Alternative sets of activities for accomplishing the various Program objectives are described and analyzed on a multiyear basis.
   - The optimum set of activities is selected from the alternatives on the basis of comparative estimated effectiveness and cost.

WESTERN NEW YORK PPBS MODEL

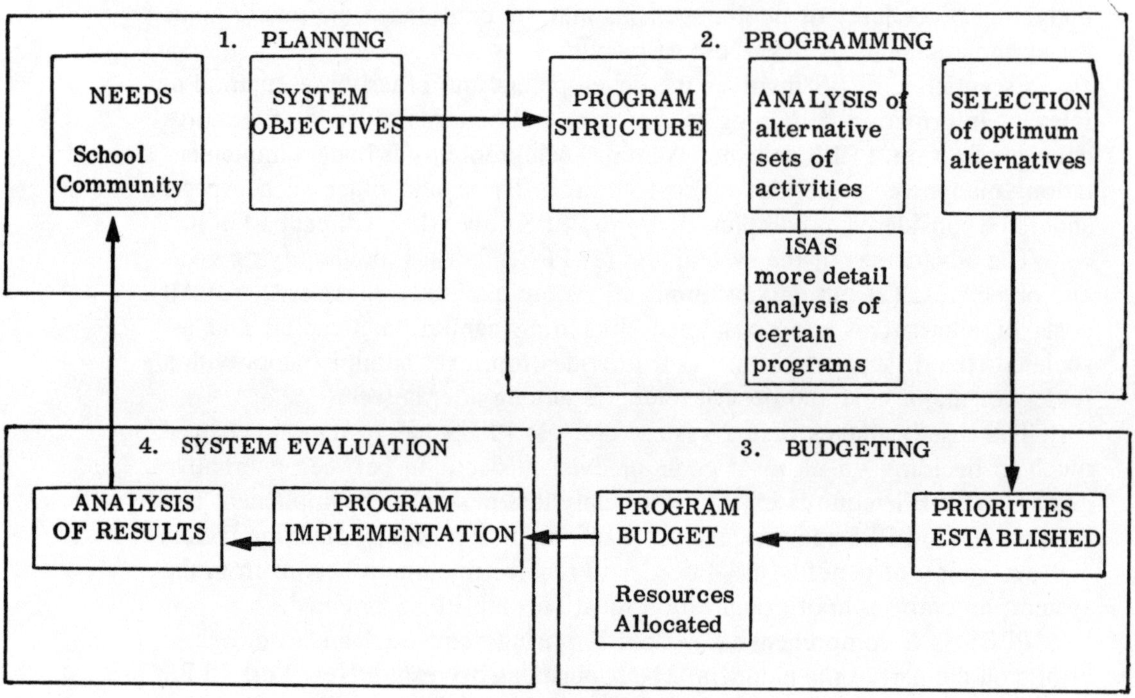

Figure 5-1

- Deficient or innovative priority Programs are subjected to more detailed analysis.
3. BUDGETING
  - Costs of achieving Program objectives via the selected set of activities are examined.
  - Funding priorities are established, based on district needs.
  - Specific Programs providing greatest achievement for most reasonable cost in *priority areas* are selected for implementation.
  - Expected results and costs of each Program for the coming year are reported to the public.
  - The public, or its representatives, authorizes the intended allocation of funds for the achievement of the results described for the district Programs.
4. SYSTEM EVALUATION
  - Achievement of Program objectives and funds expended for each Program are documented and analyzed.
  - Achievement and cost data analysis for each Program become input to the Planning and Programming functions for subsequent years.

- Achievement and cost data for each Program are reported to the public.
- Program achievement and cost data, plus continuing analysis of the community's educational needs, result in revision of objectives, Program Structure and the district's curricular Programs.

You will notice the continuous cycle of the four phases of PPBS: planning, programming, budgeting and evaluation. The cycle can be entered at any stage; however, the planning stage, during which goals and priorities are established, is a logical beginning and this is where the largest number of people should be involved.

This chapter will examine PPBS from the standpoint of how it can be applied in a school system. Special note will be taken of its advantages and disadvantages along with the current state of development of the system for school use. Specific techniques needed for its application will also be explained.

TYPICAL PROBLEMS ASSOCIATED WITH TRADITIONAL
SCHOOL DISTRICTS' BUDGETS

One of the problems which superintendents and Boards have had in presenting their budgets is that the budgets are categorical instead of programmatic. Categorical budgets are subject to categorical cuts when funds are insufficient. The effects of such cuts are not apparent and often do not show up until it is too late to do anything about them. For example, it is very difficult to analyze a budget which provides for more than a thousand teachers as a category "teachers' salaries" and contains several million dollars for the salary line. Also, such a line item does not show the true costs of teachers. In order to figure the true cost of salaries, the district categorical budget would have to be combed for such items as contributions to retirement funds, to medical plans, to social security, etc. In other words, a $10,000 per year teacher would cost more like $12,000 per year when fringe benefits are included.

From a management standpoint, it is much better to budget by cost unit tied to an objective. If funds are not available, either the objective is dropped from the program or modified with the resulting consequences immediately evident. This is an advantage of PPBS.

Supposing as an alternative to presenting a categorical budget to the school board, a cost unit by program had been presented. Consequences of budget modifications can no longer be made blindly.

To figure the true cost of a teacher unit, you would have to figure all costs associated with the hiring and maintenance of a teacher for a given year. These would include:

Salaries
Fringe benefits
Inservice education costs
Facilities costs (school maintenance)
Incidental supplies
Equipment
Textbooks and other instructional media
Supervisory services
Administrative support

Such a combination of costs then becomes a cost unit applied to any particular set of tasks. If this procedure, which is typical of PPBS systems, had been used by the district in question, it would have been easy for reviewers to recognize cost categories by program objectives if they were so grouped. Then the questions regarding program costs could be answered.

To carry the cost unit analysis one step further, assume a teacher has a base salary of $10,000. The cost unit for that teacher would likely be at least 60 to 75 percent higher when you consider all associated costs.

If you were going to put in a system of remedial reading which required ten teachers and a supervisor, the costs would be shown for all associated costs instead of categories such as salaries, tests, etc.

When the decision is made to fund or not to fund the program, the amount of money concerned becomes immediately evident.

Let's carry the remedial reading program further in this analysis.

Goal. To help every child achieve efficient reading skills within the limits of his ability.

Alternative ways to achieve the goal for the nonachieving student:

Alternative 1.   *Reduce class size* and train classroom teachers to do their own remedial work
Alternative 2.   *Hire itinerate reading specialists* for every 40 identified reading problems.
Alternative 3.   *Provide remedial aides for the regular classroom teachers* without reduction of class size.

Analysis of Costs:

Alternative 1.   Reduce class size

10 cost units @ $16,000 = $160,000

Alternative 2.   Provide itinerate reading specialists for every 40 identified children with reading problems:

8 cost units @ $17,000[1] = $136,000

Alternative 3.   Provide special remedial aides for regular classroom teachers.

40 classroom aides at unit costs of $6,000 = $240,000

In the example given, the PPBS analysis becomes clear and precise because the decision is to instigate a remedial reading program or not to instigate such a program. The selection of the best alternative from a money standpoint would appear to be Alternative 2. A complete analysis of this alternative needs to be made, however, before the final selection is made. More about this later.

This remedial program, not now in existence, would be a total new cost program and the cost-effectiveness of this additional expenditure would be ascertained by evaluation. On the other hand, in the case of ongoing integrated courses of study, the task becomes complex indeed. Take the case of elementary classroom social studies. It is part of a total curriculum with comprehensive goals, including highly generalized goals such as the teaching of citizenship.

To effectively ascertain the cost-effectiveness of this program, the goals would have to be specific. True cost units such as a certain percentage of the teacher's time and associated costs would have to be ascertained. After this is done the cost-effectiveness could be measured only if and when specific means of evaluation were developed.

This is a disadvantage of PPBS; that is, it is difficult to apply to an integrated program wherein costs are not discrete by objective. Most educators argue that educational programs are highly complex arrangements. Many of the objectives are achieved as concomitant learnings, associated with student-teacher interaction, with student interaction and with the general learning atmosphere. Many critics of PPBS are of the opinion that it simply will not work in an educational system that is highly humanistic.

There is a common misconception that PPBS is a fiscal weapon divorced from real educational concerns and centering the power of the decisions in the business office. Just the opposite is true. More power than ever is placed in the hands of educational planners, with the business relegated to an information service department, providing educators with cost estimates, data on expenditure and alternative methods of using resources. Without PPBS, business office

---

[1]Cost units are higher because reading specialists must have master's degrees and travel expenses. On the other hand, extra classrooms are not needed so that the unit cost is nearly the same.

personnel were often forced into making educational decisions because of conflicting signals from the educators.

There is also the assumption that PPBS is something superimposed from the top requiring a new breed of educational decision makers hierarchically arranged at the top. Instead, the leaders of this effort must be competently trained in education, but having mainly acquired insight into the processes of planning and with a knowledge of the language of PPBS which can be transmitted to others, the real planners. In fact, after some pervasive planning for the school system as a whole, the real power of decision rests at the "bottom" of the program, the classroom. This therefore requires the participation of everyone, including the teacher in the process.

There is no question that PPBS takes a lot of time. The question is, is it worth the time and effort? Those who favor PPBS argue that much of what we do in education is merely traditional. Planning may make us aware of the need for an educational system to accomplish certain things; PPBS may offer several alternative ways to assure these accomplishments. This is the only way educators can sensibly budget for the system. The line item, categorical negotiation approach now used is still mostly guesswork.

OPTIONS OPEN TO SCHOOL DISTRICTS

Each of the four major elements of PPBS, (1) Planning, (2) Programming, (3) Budgeting and (4) System Evaluation, is at a higher stage of development than commonly assumed by educators and the public in general. Exhaustive work has been done on each of these elements. What the system lacks is total application. Also, the application of the total system is something that cannot be achieved in a day or even a year, just as the system cannot be thoroughly presented in a single chapter of a book or even a total book.

School systems which look toward its adoption have several options.

Option 1. Adoption of components of PPBS.

This option could result in the school system using only one aspect of PPBS for a specific task. It could begin with more careful attention to the planning; that is, the preparation of needs assessments (See Chapter 2) and the generation of objectives (See Chapter 3). Accompanying those, there should be some application of the flow charting techniques to orient the staff toward thinking systematically about planning (See Chapter 4).

Option 2. Apply PPBS to specific segments of the program or only new programs.

In this case, the school system deliberately says that new programs shall be planned using PPBS. That is, if there is an evident need for a strengthened program (better spelling), or a new program which has not existed previously (a recreation program or a remedial reading program), then and only then is PPBS applied. All four elements of the process are applied: (1) the need is established and the objectives agreed upon, (2) This programming is done with alternative approaches listed, (3) The budgets are prepared according to the feasible alternatives, and (4) The selected alternative is implemented and evaluated.

Under the next option, PPBS involves only those concerned with the new program and the decisions are made systematically according to PPBS procedures.

Option 3. Long-range plan for conversion of the total system to PPBS.

This is the most radical of the options. This requires a plan for the plan. The plan itself is then generated according to the PPBS approach. The need is established and the goals are prepared, the programming is done, the budgets prepared, and the system is implemented and evaluated. Option three will require several years and will require resources specifically allocated to the purpose. The cost of Option Three is no doubt the main reason why school systems so seldom have elected this option. Where such an option is selected, state and/or federal subsidies are usually required to supplement local resources. Few local school districts are willing to invest sufficient local money into the development of a system which may be viewed as experimental, developmental and demonstrative. These kinds of programs usually demand outside resources.

Option 4. Cooperatively shared services.

Under this option several school systems go together to establish a service center on a shared cost and service basis. These cooperative centers can be established by districts banding together, with one acting as fiscal agent, or by an intermediate (county) service district or even by a state department of education. This is a highly feasible approach. This center can be governed by a joint board of educators from the cooperating districts. The services of the staff of specialists can then be made available to districts on a proportionate shared-time basis. Such a center, if equipped with a computer, can broaden its services to both the management and educational application of computers which individual districts could not afford separately. The watchwords here are "not too much diversification." Such a center could easily become overburdened with business services (computerized accounting and cooperative purchasing) to the exclusion of any possibility of providing planning services.

PROGRAM ANALYSIS

The key to putting PPBS together centers mainly on the processes involved in program analysis. This must be accomplished by the person who can facilitate decision making and give sanction to the program. Program analysis implies that there is a program or at least a plan for one, and about which a decision needs to be made regarding which alternatives to select.

The following suggested seven-step review procedure can be conducted only at such a time when all components of the plan have been completed. A guide must be prepared by the school district for this analysis review. It should be made available to planners early in the planning stage in order to assure understanding on their part of what the expectations are and what must be accomplished before the review. These recommended review steps should give assurance that each of the following seven conditions are met.

1. The specific program plan contributes to the achievement of multiyear goals of the district.
2. The objectives are in measurable terms.
3. The alternative methods of achieving objectives are considered so that the most feasible alternative can be selected for its cost-effective achievement.
4. The program requirements have been translated into resource quantities and cost requirements over a multiyear period.
5. The most feasible, cost-effective alternatives are indicated.
6. The processes can be performed under the district organization.
7. The multiyear program will fit into the curricular-fiscal plan of the district.

Let us follow through a program analysis using the seven-step analysis procedure as applied to the Remedial Reading Program mentioned earlier in this chapter.

Requirement 1. The specific program plan contributes to the achievement of the objectives of the district.

This form for analysis requires the hierarchical listing of three levels of

---

1. **Multiyear goal:**

   a. **District goal:** The district shall provide a reading program which will offer each child an opportunity to achieve a reading proficiency in keeping with his ability.

   b. **Program goal:** A remedial–corrective program shall be provided for each child who deviates more than two grade levels below his expected achievement in reading.

   c. **Course objective:** Eighty percent of students in grades four, five and six who deviate more than two grade levels below their expected reading levels shall raise their reading comprehension and skills by at least eight months per year as measured by a standard achievement instrument.

---

goals and objectives to show that the specific objective contributes to the achievement of the district and program goals.

Requirement 2. The objectives are in measurable terms.

This form requires the listing of specific measurement techniques which will indicate the effectiveness of the measurable course objective as stated in form 1.

2.   Measures of Effectiveness

Metropolitan Reading Achievement Test

   Intermediate Form A will be administered at the

beginning and Form B at the end of each year to determine

need and growth.

   As above, plus scores from the NYS normative

reading achievement test administered in December to

indicate progress.

Requirement 3. The alternative methods of achieving the objectives were considered and the most feasible alternative was indicated for its cost-effective achievement.

3.   Alternatives considered

Alternative 1. Reduce intermediate class sizes (by five)

   to 20 students and train classroom teachers to do their

   own remedial work.

Alternative 2. Hire itinerate reading specialists for every

   40 identified students who quality for remedial instruction.

Alternative 3. Provide each classroom teacher with a remedial

   aide for the regular classroom teacher, thus freeing the

   teacher to work with identified students without reduction

   of class size.

Requirement 4. The program requirements have been translated into resource quantities and cost requirements over a multiyear period.

4. Resource requirements						
Resource Categories	Alternative 1 Reduction of Class Size		Alternative 2 Itinerate Teachers		Alternative 3 Remedial Aides	
	Quantity	Cost	Quantity	Cost	Quantity	Cost
Personnel						
Administrator						
Teachers						
Teacher Aides	10 @ $16,000 per unit	$160,000			40 @ $6,000 per unit	$240,000
Reading Specialists						
Consultants	1 @ $17,000	$ 17,000	8 @ $17,000 per cost unit	$135,000		
Total Personnel		$177,000		$135,000		$240,000
Equipment						
Office furniture	1 for consul- tant @ $1,000	$ 1,000	8 for spec- ialists	$ 8,000		
Audiovisual equip.	10 classroom	$ 10,000				
Books	3 @ $ 500	$ 1,500		$ 1,500		$ 1,500
Others (study carrels)						
Total Equipment		$ 12,000		$ 9,500		$ 1,500
TOTAL		$189,000		$144,500		$241,500

Figure 5-2

This requires projection of costs. Whenever possible, the district business
office should prepare unit cost estimates for the use of planners. A teaching
unit should include salaries, benefits and support services necessary to maintain
a classroom. Unit costs can also be projected for classroom furniture, equipment, etc.

Requirement 5. The most feasible, cost-effective alternative is selected.

This form requires a statement of reasons for the support or rejection of
any alternative. Alternatives can be rejected for an insurmountable obstacle
(such as the need for ten additional classrooms which are not available) or for a
philosophical reason such as the desirability of maintaining a heterogenous
classroom unit in the intermediate grades.

5. Feasibility

Alternative 1. Reduction of class size.

This would require the reduction of five pupils per classroom unit. Since there are 40 classroom units in the district's intermediate grades (5 x 40 = 200), 200 pupils would need to be housed in new classrooms. There are not 10 classrooms available. It would require the building of one new 20-room elementary school. The plan is not feasible at this time.

Alternative 2. Itinerate teachers.

This is the least expensive of the alternatives and is logistically feasible. Philosophically, the district favors students remaining with their peers. If students are in the classroom and if the specialist is used to diagnose difficulties and consult with teachers on individualized programs, this plan is highly feasible.

Alternative 3. Remedial aides.

This plan is the most expensive of the alternatives (except for new classrooms). It does not seem to focus directly on the problem of remedial reading. Therefore, it is not recommended.

Requirement 6. The program can be performed under the district organization.

---

6.   District Organization

The itinerate reading specialists can be accommodated

by the district organization.

The coordination can be done by the elementary supervisor

and the administration can be done by the elementary principals.

Testing can be accomplished by the testing department which

already tests in the area of reading.

This requires an analysis of how the new program will fit into the district organization. If the organization cannot accommodate the new program, it should either be changed or the program must be rejected.

Requirement 7. The multiyear program will fit into the curricular-fiscal plan of the district.

---

7.   Multiyear–fiscal plan of the district

The plan will fit if annual levies are approved by the board

and the voters.

This program must be broken out as a separate program

and presented as a need. If funds are not approved the program

cannot be supported under current resources.

The example used to illustrate the systematic analysis of the feasibility of adding a new remedial program illustrates the seven steps in preparing the plan according to PPBS procedures. The application of PPBS for optional or new programs is the most feasible way for districts to introduce PPBS procedures into the district

SUMMARY

One of the responses to the criticism of wastefulness in schools and other governmental services is PPBS (Planning, Programming, Budgeting System). Essentially, PPBS involves the development and orderly presentation of relevant information pertaining to the cost and benefits of major alternative courses of action. (1) It focuses on identifying goals and objectives. (2) It looks at present and future implications of the goals. (3) Alternatives are analyzed and those which are most cost-effective are selected. (4) It provides evidence as to the most cost-effective methods of achieving the goals. (See Fig. 5-1.)

Most school budgets have traditionally been analyzed by category. When it came time to cut the budget, these cuts were often spread across categories, so much out of salaries, so much out of materials, so much out of transportation, etc. By tying costs to programs, the effects of cuts can be precisely determined, whereas the results of categorical cuts are often not known. Also, PPBS is supposed to assure that the most effective and cost-efficient alternatives have been chosen along the way. These are two of the major arguments for PPBS.

Other advantages of the system are:

1. Specific program plans contribute to the achievement of multiyear goals.
2. The objectives can be measured.
3. Alternative methods of achieving goals have been analyzed for their cost-efficiency.
4. Resource needs have been carefully planned.
5. The most feasible, cost-effective alternative has been indicated.
6. The program can be achieved in the present organization.
7. The program hits into the multiyear curricular-fiscal plan of the district.

The disadvantages of the system are:

1. It requires a costly planning staff and specialist trained in the process.
2. It was originally designed for a nonsocial operation and is difficult to apply in its purest form to a school situation.
3. It requires a carefully stated and clearly defined set of goals and objectives for the district.
4. It breaks the teaching process down into precise segments and does not always take care of those interrelated objectives known as concomitant learnings.
5. It is not understood and often resented by teachers.

This chapter recommends that all school districts consider some application of PPBS for some of their planning. This can be achieved by cooperatively establishing a shared planning service with other school districts to cut the cost of each district maintaining its own staff of specialists.

In the meantime, more development work needs to be completed before the technology of PPBS will be at the level where the system is readily applicable to all districts.

The study of PPBS can add much to any district. School leaders must keep abreast of its development and be sophisticated enough in the process to influence its refinement and also to interpret it to policy makers and law makers who otherwise might legislate it into being before its total application is feasible for all districts.

Districts can gain experience in PPBS by applying its processes to new projects and needs not already a part of the school system.

6

Developing Systematic Forecast Techniques that Predict Future Needs

Man has always tried to predict the future. Historians, philosophers and soothsayers alike, have throughout history made projections of what is to come. Many of these projections have been partly right simply because of the laws of chance, some because of wise insights. We hear much more about the lucky guesses and near misses than the totally wrong guesses. When these guesses are based upon solid knowledge of the past, a good understanding of the present, and wise inferences into the future, they can be taken out of the crystal ball category to assume the plausibility of reasonable forecasts and futures projections.

Educators deal with the future. Children are educated to function adequately in what the future will or might be. Planning of both the school program and the school facilities is based upon reasonable assumptions of what things will be like, five, ten or fifty years from now. The more nearly these assumptions are based upon sound information and reasonable alternatives, the better the planning will be.

School leaders need a knowledge of what is reasonable to expect in the future. They may rely upon instinct, judgment or some other phenomena to help them with this projection, but even the wisest of individuals needs the corroboration of other thinkers with differing information bases and the techniques of the various disciplines which they represent.

There is growing up in America a set of concerted efforts to make scientific and systematic projections of alternative future events. Scientists, government officials, business leaders and many other thoughtful people are now making a major effort to understand and forecast future social and technological developments. Often these forecasts are based on current trends, which can be projected with varying degrees of accuracy for ten, twenty or thirty years ahead. These forecasts can be helpful to those who must make the decisions needed to respond to future needs, and in fact these forecasts help planners shape future conditions to some extent. These futurist movement trends have now resulted in the establishment of the World Future Society with headquarters in Washington, D. C. and also local chapters throughout the nation. Their publication is *The Futurist*.

Knowing these forecasts is important to school leaders and planners for many reasons. Among them:

1. Better decisions can be made concerning all aspects of life to be affected by education.
2. Schools will be in a better position to lessen "future shock"—the disorientation that comes when the world changes faster than people can rearrange their thinking patterns, attitudes and values.
3. Schools can sometimes help influence the future by preparing students who are alert and responsive to new, but unforeseen circumstances.
4. It is simply good planning to have as broad an informational base as possible against which to test your assumptions.

There are three principal approaches to forecasting: the computerized projections, the Delphi Technique and the futures descriptions. This chapter will discuss these approaches and discuss their application to educational processes.

THE COMPUTERIZED APPROACH

The computerized projections utilize the new capacity for the storage and retrieval of data made possible by the computer. In computer projections, current conditions are chosen, and rates of change and direction of change are then programmed with variables introduced to ascertain their effects. Successive cycling of information into the computer will project various combinations of variables to influence the projection of any specific trends—population growth, economic conditions and sociological trends. The accuracy of the projection, of course, depends upon the ability of analysts to select the reasonable combinations of variables. For example, the phenomenal growth of IBM as a corporation at one time in the economic history of this country, if projected without modification, could have resulted in a projection that it would, in time, consume the entire economy. On the other hand, a dramatic drop in death rate, say from the conquering of cancer and heart disease, could forecast an entirely new composition of population age groups. But there would always be some unknown element which caused death that would take the places of the two dreaded killers and how they would act. If the continuation of any current trend is projected without modification or the interjection of judgments, the picture of what things will be like in the future will be skewed out of all proportions.

There are several advantages to the computerized approach, however. Among them are:

1. It is precise.
2. It responds to each individual variable or any combination of them.
3. It relies on intuition only to the extent needed to select the variables and select the combination of variables which will eventually prevail in the analysis.
4. It can easily be projected by region, country or the world as a whole.
5. It can easily be projected quantitatively.

The disadvantages of this system are:

1. The judgmental factor which is important to any projection is not particularly visible and therefore may not be recognized by the user of the data.
2. The projections are in terms of single strands of events, not total pictures of the interplay of economics on population, etc.
3. It is difficult for the user to assess the implications of the initial input into the computer.

THE DELPHI TECHNIQUE

One technique for making predictions is getting a lot of attention from educators because of its adaptability. The Delphi technique has many variations which make it particularly adaptable to getting information not only on what is anticipated to happen, but also on what is expected and desirable.

In its original form, the Delphi technique is used to forecast development and timing of future events. It relied primarily on pooled "expertise" of a number of selected authorities. A group of from 40 to 100 carefully selected experts were sent questionnaires about when they expect a certain event to occur. This is then followed up by subsequent questionnaires listing the results of the first questionnaire, etc., until there is a clear agreement among the experts on tendencies.

For example, a question may be asked about when the majority of schools will adopt the ungraded primary system of organization. The expert must estimate Before 1980—1980 to 1985—1990 to 2000—beyond the year 2000 or not at all with a reason stated. The central tendency of responses might be: 25

Event	Percentage of Probability of Event Occurring in the Year Cited		Year(s) Cited	
	Range	Median	Range	Median
2. Funding eligibility for social science curriculum projects financed by the U. S. Department of Education will include the requirement of an interdisciplinary approach.	90-90	90	71-75	73
3. Several universities provide a one-year law program for top students.	50-80	80	73-85	73
4. Educators in Switzerland demonstrate high secondary school achievement with a wide range of latency-age children (prepuberty).	60-82	80	73-77	73
7. Secondary curricula reformed and upgraded to college standards, resulting in decline of liberal arts undergraduate institutions.	20-80	80	75-90	75
22. Schools become learning resource centers characterized by itinerant personnel and independent, self-paced study.	5-95	74	71-	81
23. "Fixed periods" of instruction are replaced by flexible units of instruction focused on interdisciplinary themes, such as life, ecology, or transportation.	5-95	74	71-	81
24. A national boycott by high school students of all social science classes; reason: biased material.	10-10	10	76-90	83
38. Emphasis on cybernetics eliminates the need for much knowledge and causes adherence to principles of competition, authority and evaluation.	10-25	25	90-90	90
46. School systems become totally unstructured in order to cope with rapid change patterns.	90-95	95	1995-	1995

percent say before 1980; 50 percent say between 1980 and 1990; while 25 percent predict after 1990 or never. The second round of questionnaires lists these results and the principal reasons given. The group with this information is asked to reconsider their earlier answers in view of the information received from their counterparts. They may reaffirm their earlier prediction and state their reasons or they may be influenced to change their earlier response. Through the second and possibly the third cycle the tendency is for the group to come closer together in their predictions.

In other words, the respondents are sent a sequence of questionnaires, each one is based on the results of the last one, and each respondent therefore has the opportunity to change his views as other respondents are given him. Shown on p. 93 are some of the predictions from a Delphic survey conducted by Insgroup, Inc.[1] The entire report describes the 46 most general events, the probability of their occurring and the median predicted year at which they are expected. This particular set was compiled as the best thinking of 40 well-known educational experts. Here is one strand of their predictions selected by the author as illustrative only.

You will note by examining these predictions that some are more likely to happen than others and that some are projected to happen sooner than others.

According to this list, it is highly likely (90% chance) that "funding eligibility for social science curriculum projects financed by the U. S. Department of Education will include the requirement of an interdisciplinary approach." The anticipated date that this is expected to happen is 1973, within one year of the prediction. On the other hand, it is highly unlikely (only an estimated 10% chance) that there will be "A national boycott by high school students of all social science classes; reason: biased material." If such an event does occur, it is most likely to occur by 1983 according to this survey. Note the close agreement in probability as recorded by the range. There was absolute agreement on each of these two events in terms of probability. There was reasonably close agreement on the year for the first (71-75) and for the second citation (76-90).

For some predictions there is a reported high degree of probability, but the projection is far into the future. Note item 46. Also, for some events there is less agreement in the likelihood of an event. Note item 7 where the range is 20-80, but the median is 80. This could be interpreted to mean that most of the experts predicted the likelihood of 80%, but at least one thought the likelihood of this event happening was only 20%.

It was pointed out earlier in this discussion that the Delphi technique was developed to obtain as accurate a prediction as possible from the best and most informed groups possible. Its essential ingredient is that respondents may be

---

[1]*Predicted Educational Events*, Version IV—Results of Delphi Round No. 3, copyrighted Insgroup, Inc., 1972, One City Boulevard West, Suite 935, Orange, California 92668.

influenced through additional information from their counterparts to modify their earlier predictions. Thus each round of questionnaires becomes more and more a consensus of opinions. Its unique ingredient is recycling until close agreement is reached or until disagreements and their reasons for divergent opinions are clearly evident. Thus any technique which feeds information back and permits the participants to modify their earlier opinions may be considered an application of Delphi methods.

The process may be modified and used orally in a group meeting, or may be through written response. In Chapter 3 an oral technique was described as a means of obtaining consensus on goals. Other modified applications may be by questionnaire about such questions as:

1. Consensus opinions of parents on what schools should do about a particular problem.

2. Consensus of opinions on what the major problems are in the present school system.

3. Consensus of opinions of under what conditions parents will support increased taxes for schools.

THE DELPHI TECHNIQUE

The Delphi technique, or any one of its many modifications, has the following advantages.

1. It provides for the expression of opinions from any selected or identified group (a group of parents, a group of experts, or a group of selected opinion leaders in the community).

2. It requires reasons for the opinions expressed. (Respondents cannot simply say "yes" or "no" without stating a reason.)

3. It recycles the process to provide for evermore refined data. (The second and third opportunities help the respondent to rethink his earlier opinion.)

4. It gives respondents an opportunity to modify their earlier opinion based on data received from other respondents. (On the basis of data supplied, a new consideration may modify the earlier opinion.)

5. It leads toward consensus of opinion. (Ninety percent agree that students will demand more participation in curriculum selection within five years.)

6. It gives planners data on which to plan. (The public may be more receptive to the idea of change than anticipated.)

7. It gives administrators a basis of providing information to those who help in planning. (The Board of Education can be informed that 80 percent of the survey group agreed that career education needs more emphasis.)

8. It alerts administrators to problem areas in communications to which

they should respond. (An increased public information effort is needed if most parents have misinformation about their schools.)

9. It may on occasions point out trends which should be counteracted if such trends are considered detrimental. (An increased emphasis on drug education, if it is predicted that drug use will become more prevalent.)
10. It may alert administrators to the need for alternative action to counteract the inevitable. (A campaign for more state aid if taxpayers are predicted to refuse to vote more funds.)

THE ALTERNATIVE FUTURES APPROACH

The alternative futures approach of forecasting puts the predications in the context of certain collections of trends.

The alternative futures approach is a highly technical approach to planning. It depends upon a group of scholars who look sociologically at certain trends and predict where these trends might lead the country or world. The scholars then write scenarios or descriptions of what society will be like if certain trends converge at certain points in the future.

The alternative futures approach does not predict which future is most likely, but it only points to alternative pictures of what the world might be like if certain combinations of trends come together. It is up to the planner then to make his decisions based upon whichever scenario he selects and his predictions of how this will affect him, his business or his profession. So far, the alternative futures writers have not reduced their scenarios to specific trends for the automotive industry, medicine or schools, for example. They simply have given the user the descriptions and let him do his own analysis of what things could be like.

The Northwest Regional Educational Laboratory projected, with the assistance of some specialists, five scenarios of possible alternative futures as a basis of their planning for their Rural Education Program. Since the program was designed to assist rural people in planning the kinds of schools they need and want for their children, it only seemed reasonable to look critically at what the world could be like five, ten or twenty years from now, points at which the results of the program would likely have their greatest impact on rural communities.

It was reasoned that this approach, together with information from Delphi surveys and computer projections, would identify those elements in our society which most likely would influence trends in rural communities. Computer projections alone might lead to the conclusion that there would be no rural communities left if the movement to cities and suburbs continued at rates established in the 50's and 60's. One of the characteristics of rurality is the element of isolation. Would this continue or indeed reverse itself? Could communities plan in such a way as to influence what will happen to them? Could they attract small compatible industries and still maintain their life-styles? These and other questions needed the best answers available before the program plans were put into final form. A consultant was engaged to work with the program team to project alternative futures scenarios. These scenarios were based on the work done by the Educational Policy Research Center of Stanford Research Institute. Here are some excerpts from the five scenarios:

Excerpts from Scenario I, Mild New Left

This pattern, starting from a mild "new left" position, is one characterized by an aura of ineptitude, although this feeling will be some time in developing. Certain characteristics of the youth movement are assumed to be amplified, namely the observable contempt for material goods and for technical skills, the feeling that current productivity is sufficient *and* (incompatibly) a commitment to the erasure of poverty in the U.S. and its ameliorization in hungrier countries. The incompatibility of these feelings will lead to overextension and failure, with disillusionment coming as a primary result and a shortage of technical skills growing from the disillusionment.

It goes on to include:

- A recession of substantial proportions is likely.
- Governmental control of the economy in an effort to combat and stem the recession would be called for.
- Attention to basic human issues such as ecology and social balance would diminish of necessity.
- Foreign policy in this set of circumstances would quickly move into an isolationist position.
- Rural poverty would deepen and the migration to the cities would only enlarge the problems characteristic to the urban scene.

Excerpts from Scenario II, Hostile Pluralism

The second case also grows out of the assumption that the "new left" attitude is a reasonable way of looking at the present. This case is one in which an increasing discontent with the prevailing state of affairs on different sides of society—principally by the young and the poor—has produced a fragmentation of values and aspirations among the populace of the United States. This arrangement of many positions may be called a "hostile pluralism"—but with a significant and unique characteristic due to its "new left" influence: the thrust toward pluralism is a positive action, and fragmentation is an approved action rather than a disapproved reaction. High value is placed on plural difference.

It goes on to include:

- The varying factions are multifold and mutually antagonistic to greater or lesser degrees with a strongly participatory or direct form of democracy.
- Economic influences lie in the sphere of conservative development which treats major problems with an excess of caution.
- The pollution problem will have muddled its way to a stalemate.
- If the trend toward factionalism—the entropic tendencies of a volatile or restive society—is allowed to continue without attention, a situation similar to France's Fourth Republic will be likely to follow.

Excerpts from Scenario III, Mild Right-Wing

The third pattern can be called a mild right-wing control scene. There will be a moderate to conservative feeling in the country which could lead to a kind of mediocre but steady growth, but there might also be a pervasive downturning of everything. This would lead to a progressively defensive attitude toward the world, with shutdown, withdrawal, and perhaps a more authoritarian set of controls. It is a long-term conservative situation with a recessionist flavor, and isolationism vis-a-vis developing countries. Nationalization of industries may begin to develop.

It goes on to include:

- The "silent majority" will exert more pressure to cause society to conform to its mode.
- A wall will be built around America and the North Atlantic Community, and attention will be turned to internal problems in a cautious but pragmatic way.
- There will be a fallback on community patterns in any hard-time circumstance, rather than a creative solution to problems; learning will have a distinctly utilitarian tone.

Excerpts from Scenario IV, Mid-Course Mode

A plausible world pattern which is less spectacular than the first two "ineptitude" patterns and less depressing than the third pattern is a mid-course mode which is largely an extension of the current state of things. This, like the third pattern, will be basically a "tame" situation. If anything, this society will be marked by a retreat to American issues, a close-to-the-vest approach to both internal growth and external influence, and a stalemate on issues of national demand such as pollution and social flexibility. It will be seen again that the silent majority is larger and more powerful than anyone had suspected, and it is the views of this so-called silent majority which will dominate and will determine national policies.

It goes on to include:

- There will be a continuing growth of the economy, but at rates that will be moderate at best.
- The government will be most likely be marked by a further decentralization.
- This prospective world pattern, growing as it does out of the *status quo* in a natural extension, may be the one which will appeal to the greatest number of people.

Excerpts from Scenario V, War on Ecological Imbalance

The fifth and final alternative world pattern is seen as an outgrowth of an early and successful assault on a problem of national significance. An apt candidate for this sort of assault would be a massive "war" on the ecological imbalance which currently threatens the stability of the world culture. A successful and concerted attack on the problem of ecological imbalance could be expected to have the effect of producing a renewed vigor in the national spirit, as the problem proved under attack to be a smaller problem than had been thought.

It goes on to include:

- The renewed exuberance and vigor in spirit that would emerge from a successful assault on some national problem would be characterized by feelings of richness and confidence.
- The United States would tend to maintain its worldwide sphere of influence both militarily and through economic aid.
- Two different modes of activity could eventuate from a boom period of this kind. One mode would be a society of satisfied prosperity which would be liable to "sag" and lose momentum in following decades. The other likely alternative would be an authoritarian prosperity with a cybernetic twist, a society that would contain the germ of an Orwellian theocracy as it gradually moved from a sense of confidence toward a protective stance regarding its riches.

These scenarios were then analyzed by the program team for their potential effect upon rural life and, specifically, rural schools. Common elements were identified, trends were projected and issues to address were selected. This was one application of the alternative futures approach applied to a specific planning problem.

So far, alternative futures descriptions have never been disseminated broadly. The scenarios tend to be highly technical with very fine differences which are hard to keep in mind as one goes from one to another.

The authors of scenarios talk of the necessity of the user to "internalize" the data. That is, he must be familiar with the scenarios, the fine differences among them and use his own judgment of their plausibility. They thus become a part of his "perceptive mass" or things in his head which influence his judgment as he considers specific new decisions.

However, it remains for educational scholars to use the scenarios currently developed to develop clearer pictures of what the alternative futures mean to educational planning. This is yet to be done.

The alternative futures approach to prediction has the following advantages.

1. They are scholarly predictions based upon projections of current or alternative trends into the future.
2. They provide broad descriptions of what things might be like based upon conjectured combinations of trends merging at certain intervals.
3. They are presented in scenarios (or descriptions) of what things can be like if certain elements come together.
4. They broaden the view of the reader as to what might come to pass.

Alternative futures use by educators at its current state of development has the following disadvantages.

1. It does not estimate the likelihood of one alternative over another.
2. It is based upon fine differences which are difficult to discern from the scenarios.
3. It is not currently broken down for its possible effect on such institutions as education.
4. It leaves to the reader the requirement of making his own projection as to what effects different combinations of events will have upon his primary concern (in this case, education).
5. It seems to convey in inevitableness of trends which could entrap mankind into certain sets of conditions over which he has little or no control. He thus may perceive his destiny as fate instead of a set of circumstances over which he has some control.
6. It requires the reader to read and reread the scenarios until he "internalizes" them in such a way as to make them part of his thinking.

SUMMARY

There is a need for those in educational leadership positions to know as much as possible about what may come to pass. Teachers, too, will benefit from this knowledge. It will help teachers and planners to make wiser judgments in selecting the most imperative problems to work on, to select the best and most needed goals and objectives for their instructional programs, and finally to gear up to meet anticipated rough spots as they proceed along the path of educational planning, instructing and evaluating.

This chapter discussed three major techniques used in long-range projections of alternative futures.

The first discussed was the computerized techniques. These techniques are based upon current trends by extending the lines of the present into the future. The lines were not modified by the interjection of variables, which in the judgment of the analysts might affect or modify the trends. It looks like Figure 6-1.

COMPUTERIZED EXTENSION OF CURRENT TRENDS

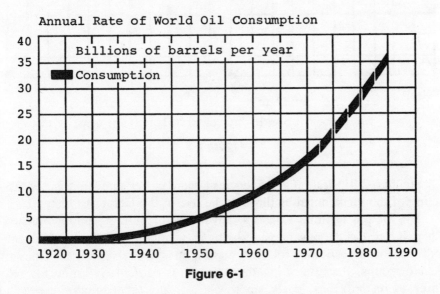

Figure 6-1

Figure 6-1 illustrates the importance of the judgmental factor in modifying trends into the future. For example, oil consumption, if projected at the present rate, would increase alarmingly. Such variables as the following have not been taken into consideration: reduction in speed limits to 50 miles per hour; trend toward smaller cars; more moderate room temperatures; increased use of other sources of energy, etc. Any one of these variables could be estimated and programmed into the computer. The reader often does not know, however, which modifying variables have gone into the final projection. This is one of the drawbacks of computerized projections.

The second technique discussed in this chapter was the Delphi technique.

This is a technique for getting expert opinion as to the likelihood of any particular event happening and, if so, when. Its main advantage is that it depends on ever finer judgments as the information about the surveys is recycled to the judgment group.

DELPHI TECHNIQUE TOWARD CONSENSUS

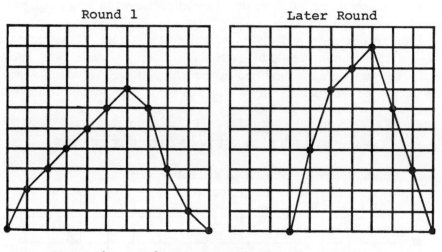

Round 1   Later Round

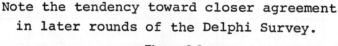

Note the tendency toward closer agreement
in later rounds of the Delphi Survey.

Figure 6-2

Figure 6-2 illustrates the tendencies toward closer agreement in successive cycling of the questionnaires through the use of the Delphi technique.

The Delphi technique has the advantage of pulling opinions closer together. It also has the advantage of being an adaptable technique which can be modified for the eliciting of information in successive rounds from only selected groups. Because of its adaptability it is particularly useful for getting consensus on priorities, goals, approaches or any other opinion-based judgments.

The third approach discussed in this chapter was the Alternative Futures projections. These word pictures of various scenes from the future are made by scholars who study the potential alternatives of what the world will look like five, ten or twenty years from now if various combinations of events come together.

Figure 6-3 is explained by the Stanford Research Institute[2] as follows:

---

[2]Stanford Research Institute, *Futures Projection in Support of Executive Decision*, p. 8, copyright 1972

PLANNING CONE

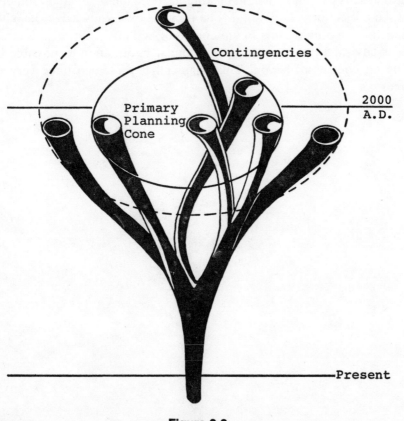

Figure 6-3

When . . . a set [of contenders] is selected, it can be thought of as a "tree" as shown here. In this tree, each projection is presented by a "tube," which takes its own individual route away from the present but which is described in terms that are similar to ones that would be used for describing the present.

The "planning cone" (superimposed on the tree illustrated here) is delineated by those traces of events that are judged to be just marginally plausible. By definition, all traces lying completely within or along the boundaries of the planning cone would be worthy of consideration.

The authors of the futures scenarios emphasize the usefulness of their projection only to the extent that the word pictures are read, understood and "internalized" by the reader. It then becomes part of the reader's thinking patterns.

All of the projection techniques presented in this chapter rely upon judgment of the projectionist. These judgments are just that. It remains for the reader to use his own judgment in making his decision based upon some, all or part of the projections. In doing this he uses his own knowledge, insights and intuitions in determining this future course of action.

It is advisable, however, to get as much information as possible before deciding on courses of action. This chapter has presented three very useful resources.

7

Preparing People for Change—The Force Field Analysis Technique

It would be foolish to attempt to achieve a significant change in any system, let alone one as complex as a school system, without first assessing the potential to succeed. Whether the desired change be for the better use of supplies or for something more encompassing—like restructuring of the attendance areas for a large school system—change will have an impact on people.

Most people within an organization want, at the onset, to know two things about change. First, they want to know where they will fit in the new plan. (Who will be over me or under me in the organizational hierarchy?) Second, they want to know how the new plan will affect their ability to do their work. (Will I be expected to do more? Can I do it? Will the new plan slow me down? Will I have what I need to work with?)

You, as an administrator, will need to gather and analyze data about how people *feel* about the proposed changes before initiating them. We can all name numerous examples of good plans that fell short of expectations because of failure to account for the human elements. It is unfortunate when we learn, *after* installing a new plan, that people didn't want the change, they wouldn't or couldn't do what was expected, or they didn't understand the reasons for the change.

This chapter will deal only with the *feeling aspect* of planned change. Questions you will be considering here are:

1. Will the plan be accepted by the people involved?
2. How can I, as a school administrator, find out how people really feel about the plan?
3. How can I influence these feelings?

These attitudes and perceptions of the people affected will constitute most of the human *forces for* or *against* the plan and thus they can spell success or failure for your effort.

A powerful technique for systematically looking at these human forces is the *force field analysis technique*. This technique, like many others used in educational planning, was borrowed from the physical sciences. The idea is that any situation is as it is at any given time because of counterbalanced forces (Figure 7-1).

COUNTERBALANCED FORCES

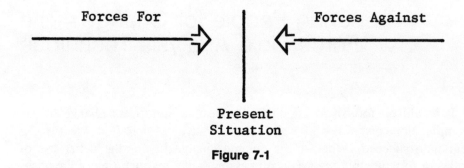

Figure 7-1

If the situation is in equilibrium, the forces are presumed to be in balance and opposite, cancelling each other. If, on the other hand, one or more forces should be modified, the situation would be expected to change. Change in position of any force will, according to the theory, always result in a change in the situation (Figure 7-2).

CHANGING FORCES

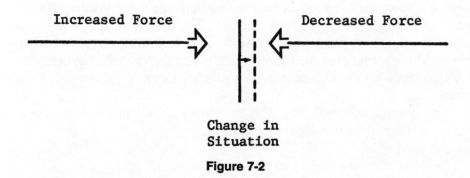

Figure 7-2

When a change begins it can be relatively slow or alarmingly rapid. An alert administrator is aware of the rapidity with which situations can change and attempts to influence them in the preferable direction.

The following illustrations depict how the force field analysis technique can be used to solve problems in education. The first case is an application of the technique to a situation within a single school; the second application treats a complex situation arising out of the needs of a large school system.

The teachers in Adams School had to order their own supplementary classroom books because there was no full-time librarian and very little clerical help available. Their dissatisfaction over this stemmed from the fact that much duplication existed in the purchase orders and that they never knew what books other teachers already had in their rooms which could have been borrowed. Some teachers had ordered books only to find that several copies already existed in the school and further, that the pupils didn't like some of the books they ordered.

Why, you might ask, was such an inefficient and unsatisfactory system in existence? Yet it did exist and there were indeed counterbalancing forces which maintained it.

THE BOOK ORDERING PROCEDURE

Forces For $\implies$	Forces Against $\impliedby$
It has always been done this way.	Duplication of purchase orders was evident.
It provided maximum freedom of choice on the part of teachers.	It was difficult to assure selection of only the best books.
It provided minimum "fuss and bother" about the procedure.	Duplication of materials existed.
It didn't require much clerical help.	There was a limitation to the number of titles available to a classroom because of duplication.

Figure 7-3

A solution to the problem might have been for the principal to suggest that a new plan be designed. He might have appointed a committee of teachers who, after looking at the system, could have recommended that the book ordering procedure permit purchase only from standard catalogs which list only those books recommended by responsible national sources of review, thereby overcoming poor selection. The committee could have recommended further that there be a school central catalog of all books on hand so that teachers ordering books could check to see how many were already on hand. Finally, they could have recommended a pooling of ownership among the rooms, thus permitting students to have broader exposure to the books available in the school.

What were the chances, according to a force field analysis, of the new book acquisition plan being accepted and maintained by the faculty of Adams School?

In the force field analysis technique, you simply begin by writing down in two opposite columns the *forces for* and the *forces against* the new plan being successful. For example, the new plan would make more books available to students over a year's time. Teachers would agree that this is desirable. Thus, this is a force *for* the procedure being adopted and should be written on the left side of the page. On the other hand, it would require that the books be exchanged at intervals. Since the teachers wouldn't like the necessity of accounting for the books, boxing them up and exchanging them, this would be a *force against*. (See Figure 7-4.)

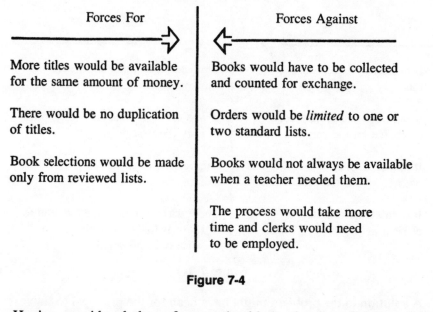

SHOULD THE NEW BOOK PURCHASE
PLAN BE ADOPTED?

Forces For	Forces Against
More titles would be available for the same amount of money.	Books would have to be collected and counted for exchange.
There would be no duplication of titles.	Orders would be *limited* to one or two standard lists.
Book selections would be made only from reviewed lists.	Books would not always be available when a teacher needed them.
	The process would take more time and clerks would need to be employed.

Figure 7-4

Having considered these forces, should the faculty of Adams School initiate a new book ordering procedure? Not without a lot more work; there are too many forces against it. Teachers would complain, would not be on time with their exchanges, and eventually the new procedure would break down for lack of support within the faculty, unless it were maintained on the authority basis. The authority basis alone is difficult to maintain over a period of time and always eventually breaks down in a system of human beings.

An alternative to an authority basis would be to analyze and discuss the force field analysis chart with teachers to check the original perceptions of the analyst and to clarify the issues. If the perceptions were correct as checked by the analyst, then all would understand why the decision was not to adopt a new procedure but to live with a modification of the old procedure. The probable result would be more effort on the part of teachers to do a good job in selecting books and voluntarily exchanging books. The net result would be less beefing about the old procedure. Each person then would know what data were used in reaching a decision, how the decision was checked, what the alternatives were and why the decision was made as it was.

The above illustration—the problem of ordering books—was a relatively simple one, but certainly not unimportant. It was confined to a narrow population, the teachers in one school, and it was an issue which did not involve too many conflicting interests and goals of high emotional impact.

The force field analysis technique is one of many techniques included in the Research Utilizing Problem Solving training system, developed and tested by the Northwest Regional Educational Laboratory.[1]

We will now employ the force field analysis technique to evaluate a much more complex situation. Middleville was an old community with changing school populations and changing attendance patterns. Some schools were old and a new building was needed to replace an old one. As an alternative plan to replacing the old school with a new building, the Board of Education and the Administration agreed to adopt a new set of boundary lines among schools to utilize space better and at the same time to close the obsolete building. The educators felt that the following goals were also within the plan's capabilities:

1. Adjusting attendance to reasonable capacity within all schools, thus eliminating the necessity of replacing the obsolete building.
2. Reducing racial imbalance among the schools by redrawing attendance lines.
3. Holding busing to a minimum, thus reducing inconvenience and cost and yet achieving better balance.

You, as administrators, are faced daily with just such complex problems. What, then, are the chances of the above goals being achieved successfully and with a minimum of disruption to faculty, children, parents and school administrators?

Obviously, the force field analysis technique will be only a beginning, but by extending its steps it can evolve into a constructive, positive procedure for achieving the goals.

In the example just given, the superintendent began by making a force field analysis chart. He listed in the two opposite columns the forces *for* and the forces *against* this program being successful. He began with those forces he *assumed* to be present.

---

[1]Commercial Educational Distributing Services, P.O. Box 3711, Portland, Oregon 97208.

The apparent forces for and against the new plan's success appeared as in Figure 7-5.

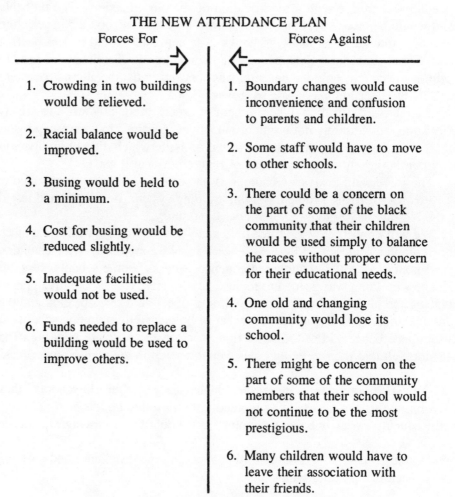

THE NEW ATTENDANCE PLAN

Forces For	Forces Against
1. Crowding in two buildings would be relieved.	1. Boundary changes would cause inconvenience and confusion to parents and children.
2. Racial balance would be improved.	2. Some staff would have to move to other schools.
3. Busing would be held to a minimum.	3. There could be a concern on the part of some of the black community that their children would be used simply to balance the races without proper concern for their educational needs.
4. Cost for busing would be reduced slightly.	
5. Inadequate facilities would not be used.	4. One old and changing community would lose its school.
6. Funds needed to replace a building would be used to improve others.	5. There might be concern on the part of some of the community members that their school would not continue to be the most prestigious.
	6. Many children would have to leave their association with their friends.

Figure 7-5

CHECKING PERCEPTIONS

Before starting a public information campaign, the superintendent needed more data. An informal approach to checking his perceptions appeared preferable. Therefore, he first talked informally to representatives of several groups involved regarding the major areas of concern. These then became:

1. Crowding: How important is it and to whom?
2. Racial Balance: How do the black and white people feel about it?
3. Busing: How strong an issue is this?
4. Teacher Transfers to Another Building: Is this an important concern?

5. Pupil Transfers to Another Building: Do pupils really care very much about this?
6. Will support personnel (noneducators) be affected?
7. Loss of School in a Neighborhood: Do people care?

The superintendent checked these issues with an available group, in this case, building administrators. They confirmed all the issues except the issue regarding teacher transfers, which they didn't consider important.

The building administrators then identified some opinion leaders (individuals around whom others seem to center to discuss issues and whose opinions were sought by others) with whom the superintendent could talk further. These individuals, they felt, would tend to speak with greater insight on general attitudes than others.

The superintendent left the building administrators with the names of parents, of teachers, of pupils and of community leaders with whom he should talk.

Much of the work of talking with people was accomplished by telephone, some in small groups over coffee, and some by face-to-face discussion.

He found that each force listed was indeed a real issue. Some were more important than others and some could be broken down into several substatements. For example, the teachers *were* worried about being transferred. This was contrary to the opinions of the principals. In fact, some of the teachers did not trust the principals and had assumed that the principals might arbitrarily transfer all teachers whom they didn't like to different schools. Of course, they couldn't tell the principals this, but were willing to discuss the problem when invited to do so with the superintendent. Teacher concerns about transfers, then, became a subissue, worthy of a force field of its own. (See Figure 7-6.)

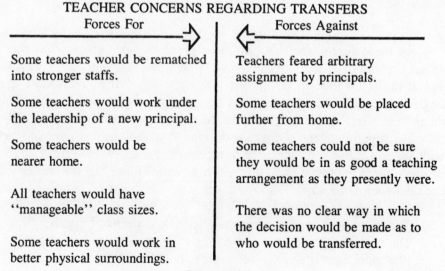

TEACHER CONCERNS REGARDING TRANSFERS

Forces For	Forces Against
Some teachers would be rematched into stronger staffs.	Teachers feared arbitrary assignment by principals.
Some teachers would work under the leadership of a new principal.	Some teachers would be placed further from home.
Some teachers would be nearer home.	Some teachers could not be sure they would be in as good a teaching arrangement as they presently were.
All teachers would have "manageable" class sizes.	There was no clear way in which the decision would be made as to who would be transferred.
Some teachers would work in better physical surroundings.	

Figure 7-6

Some of these forces were more important than others. The next step was to rearrange them in the order of importance. This, then, became a categorical list as shown in Figure 7-7.

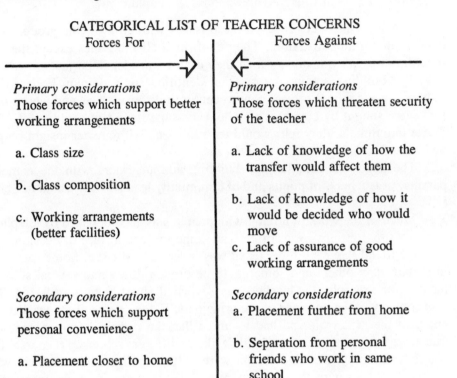

CATEGORICAL LIST OF TEACHER CONCERNS

Forces For	Forces Against
Primary considerations Those forces which support better working arrangements	*Primary considerations* Those forces which threaten security of the teacher
a. Class size	a. Lack of knowledge of how the transfer would affect them
b. Class composition	
c. Working arrangements (better facilities)	b. Lack of knowledge of how it would be decided who would move
	c. Lack of assurance of good working arrangements
Secondary considerations Those forces which support personal convenience	*Secondary considerations* a. Placement further from home
a. Placement closer to home	b. Separation from personal friends who work in same school
b. Chance to work in a new facility	

Figure 7-7

As these forces for this particular problem were analyzed, it became apparent that a plan of action should be undertaken to lessen the *forces against* and at the same time to strengthen the *forces for*. All of the forces against tended to center around the need for assurances as to fair and impartial procedures to be used in deciding who would transfer and who would not.

The superintendent in this case decided to appoint a committee of teachers with administrative representation to recommend a set of criteria which should be used in making transfers of teachers to new facilities. The committee was to consider such issues as:

1. The balance of staff to meet the educational needs of pupils.
2. The balance of staff to achieve teams which work well together.
3. Personnel convenience issues which should be considered:
   a) Seniority of teacher.

b) Personal wishes of teachers.

c) Amount of notice to be given teachers before transfer.

d) Procedure to be used if teachers object to being transferred.

The plan, then, as far as teacher personnel were concerned, was:

1. To involve teachers in the decision-making process to help them feel a part of the process.
2. To put teachers and administrators on committees together so that more trust would be promoted.
3. To direct the committee's attention to a specific set of issues to assure that the broadest aspects of the problem were considered, e.g., the welfare of pupils as well as the welfare of teachers.
4. To direct the committee to recommend to the superintendent a set of criteria for transfer, reserving for him the right to make the final decisions for which he would be held accountable.

PARENT/COMMUNITY CONCERNS

Another concerned population was made up of parents and the district as a whole. Procedures for obtaining their opinions and influencing them are uncertain. Sometimes the visible leaders, such as PTSA presidents, are not the opinion leaders of the community. According to some research on power structures of communities, depending on size, the following sectors are in descending orders of influence upon community decision making. [2]

1. Newspaper editors and publishers
2. Presidents of large banks
3. Physicians
4. Owners of a large business
5. President or executive of the Chamber of Commerce
6. Outstanding lawyer in the community
7. Women active in social activities
8. Old line politicians
9. County commissioners
10. Ministers of large churches
11. Political party leaders
12. County agents (farm)
13. Well known union leaders
14. School superintendent
15. Recognized leader of Negro community

---

[2]James Longstreth, "Guide for Administrators—Knowing Who's Who in 'Power Structure' Can Pay Dividends," *The American School Board Journal*, August 1966.

In this case study the superintendent looked at cross-sections of the community in an effort to obtain a balanced committee of eight or ten people who could be endorsed by the Board of Education as an advisory committee.

To help him make a reasonable selection of committee members, he used the categories of influential individuals listed. These individuals should also be:

1. Members of a community affected by the proposed change.
2. Willing to serve.
3. Credible in the eyes of others in the community.
4. Representative of more than one category of parents (when feasible).
5. Representative of a balance of those affected (men-women; black-white; lower and upper socioeconomic; neighborhood to lose the school and neighborhood to receive transfers).

Highest priority was to be given to parents of children to be affected by the transfer. Names in this case study were obtained informally by the superintendent. His typical conversations went like this.

> Henry, I'm looking for someone who lives in the Adams, Irvington, Whitman or Washington school areas who has a child in school and is from the banking community. You are a banker. Can you name two or three respected individuals who would fit this description who might be willing to give us some advice on some school planning that we are doing?

This approach has several things to recommend it. It was informal and friendly. It involved more people by including in the process those who do the nominating as well as those who are finally selected. It made no preliminary commitment to those being considered. It provided time for deliberation.

Through this nomination approach the superintendent was able to establish selection procedures and enter names on a list as he deliberated in his attempts to select a balanced committee.

The selection of the advisory group emerged as a compromise of the many influences. The power of such a group will always be in proportion to their ability to interpret the concerns of their reference groups (the group with which they are identified). Therefore, the superintendent must get those who not only are close to the norms of the group they represent, but also are opinion leaders in the groups.

The committee in this case study emerged as follows:

> Mr. Jones: A banker and member of the Chamber of Commerce who has a child in Adams School.

Mr. Thornton: A black attorney who is a member of NAACP, and who has a child in Irvington School.

Mrs. Smith: A PTSA president of Whitman School with a child attending there, and also a member of the League of Women Voters.

Mrs. James: A parent of a child in Washington School, on the PTSA City Council, and has been a councilwoman in city government.

Mr. Samuelson: A parent of a child in Adams School, a businessman and influential in politics.

Mrs. Fletcher: A parent of a child in Washington district, active in the Professional Women's Association, and an executive in charge of personnel for the County Commission.

Mr. Walters: A former parent in Whitman area, a labor leader and a member of the opposite political party committee.

Mrs. Phelps: A black parent in the Washington area, a registered nurse and a recognized women's leader in the Council of Churches.

All categories of influence could not be represented because of location and the community composition. The selection of the final committee became a tradeoff. Certain criteria were more important than others. Also, the credibility of the members loomed higher than any other consideration. The selection procedures thought about in advance by the superintendent had many advantages. They *required* him to consider each item; therefore his decisions were conscious ones made for valid reasons—not by chance.

The advisory committee, after its sanction by the Board of Education, was ready to begin work with the superintendent.

By using the force field analysis technique with the advisory committee, the superintendent was able to keep the purpose of the committee explicit and before them at all times. The committee soon became a task force to analyze the feasibility of the plans according to the feelings of people. Being a group of known opinion leaders, their opinions had a high degree of credibility. A random group, on the other hand, would only have been able to give their assumptions and would not have been able to speak for their sector. In the force field analysis technique, the ability of the group to check original perceptions is all important; therefore, the careful selection of participants according to a systematic procedure was essential.

With such a representative, credible committee, the superintendent in this example was able to discuss each issue frankly. Committee interaction and discussion clarified the issues and helped categorize them into a highly reliable set of conditions which were of real concern.

The force field chart, after refinement, emerged as Figure 7-8.

CATEGORICAL FORCES FOR AND AGAINST
A REDISTRICTING PLAN WORKING
(Parents and Community)

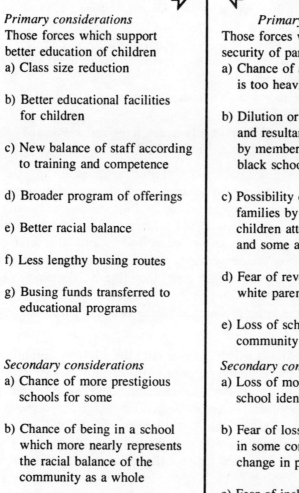

Forces For → ← Forces Against

Primary considerations
Those forces which support
better education of children
a) Class size reduction

b) Better educational facilities
   for children

c) New balance of staff according
   to training and competence

d) Broader program of offerings

e) Better racial balance

f) Less lengthy busing routes

g) Busing funds transferred to
   educational programs

Secondary considerations
a) Chance of more prestigious
   schools for some

b) Chance of being in a school
   which more nearly represents
   the racial balance of the
   community as a whole

c) Redirecting building funds to
   improve all facilities

Primary considerations
Those forces which threaten
security of parents
a) Chance of a racial balance which
   is too heavily white or black

b) Dilution or spread of identity
   and resultant loss of power
   by members of predominantly
   black schools

c) Possibility of breaking up
   families by having some
   children attend one school
   and some another

d) Fear of reverse busing by
   white parents

e) Loss of school in one
   community

Secondary considerations
a) Loss of most prestigious
   school identity

b) Fear of loss of property value
   in some communities by
   change in population

c) Fear of inability of children
   getting into college

d) Fear of loss of community
   identity

e) Fear of introduction of new
   "less academic programs in
   new schools"

Figure 7-8

Again, as in the case of teachers, parents' concerns tended to cluster around need for assurance of a good education for their children and the fear of the unknown. These forces against tended to cluster around the need for a set of assurances to alleviate the fear of the unknown. Not all of these could be dealt with by the superintendent and school board alone; e.g., the possibility of property value loss if districts were changed. But a clear set of issues gave the plan a fighting chance of success if a positive program of action could be undertaken.

Actions indicated at this point should include the establishment of community discussion groups, perhaps handled by school principals, with the assistance of a representative of the advisory committee to explain plans for boundary lines, staffing, educational programs, learning environments, bus routes and other concerns.

By following this procedure the superintendent had an excellent chance of succeeding in the plan. The positive (forces for) were emphasized and the negative (forces against) were explained with strategy committees appointed. For example, one committee came up with the idea of selecting neighborhood advisory committees to help each school implement the plan. Another plan was to provide for administrative transfers as needed for a period of five years to assure families that their children could all go to the same school. These were good suggestions; they were implemented and they made the difference between success and organized community opposition to the plan.

This case study illustrates the power of the *force field analysis technique* to lead to constructive plans of action in assuring success of educational improvement efforts.

SUMMARY

The essential features of the force field analysis technique have, through these examples, been illustrated. The technique, it was pointed out earlier in this chapter, is based on a theoretical construct borrowed from the physical sciences. The principal ideas are as follows:

1. Any set of conditions exists because of counterbalancing forces *for* and *against*.
2. An equilibrium is maintained as long as the forces remain equal on both sides.
3. When a condition is at rest, the counterbalancing forces are assumed to be constant.
4. When a single force changes, movement of the condition will result.
5. Velocity of the movement from center is determined by the power and number of new forces for or against the present conditions.

If conditions are to be changed (improved) by school leaders, existing forces which maintain the present conditions must necessarily be disturbed. Such interference should be undertaken only after a careful analysis of the force field to anticipate where interventions must be made to shore up the structure. To do less is like removing the props from under a bridge without knowing whether it can continue to stand.

In applying the force field analysis technique to planned change, the following are important guidelines to remember:

1. The force field should be analyzed by setting down, in opposite columns, those forces for or against any change being successful.
2. The forces should be specific—never general.
3. The forces should represent the feelings of as many groups or individuals as consider themselves concerned with the issue.
4. The first set of forces is based on perceptions of what exists or will exist.
5. These perceptions are tested by discussion with those concerned.
6. The testing must be with all parties concerned personally or by credible representatives of the groups.
7. Forces should be analyzed according to priority (those most important and those least important).
8. Planned intervention should be made to increase those forces *for* the desired program and to lessen those forces *against* the program's success.

8

How to Influence Public Opinion— Ten Principles for a Good Public Information Program

If one looked only at the number of school budgets defeated, one would conclude that the public in general had little confidence in their schools. Despite the many problems in public schools as reported in the media, the public still feels that schools are providing a better education now than they did a generation ago.

According to responsible opinion polls,[1] there are inconsistencies in the public's attitude, however. They do not seem to grasp the significance of relationship between small class sizes and cost, for example. This conflict is evident from answers to such questions as, "Would smaller class sizes improve education?" on the one hand, and "Would extra expenditures over and above average costs improve education?" The majority of parents responded that small class sizes were needed, but that increased funds would not improve education.

This incongruity illustrates very well that the public has a great deal of awareness of schools in general but very little awareness of the cause and effect of good school programs.

Early school public relations programs were modeled closely after advertising efforts in industry. These efforts relied heavily upon making the public more aware of their schools and putting only positive images before them.

Typically, advertisers employ such techniques as glib generalities—"The American Way;" or transfer of prestige—"Endorsed by the American Council

---

[1]George H. Gallup, "Fifth Annual Gallup Poll of Public Attitudes Toward Education," *Phi Delta Kappan*. Vol. LV, No. 1, September 1973, pp. 38-50.

of Economics;'' testimonials—''Joe Smith, the noted scientist, found the program beneficial.'' Altogether, these techniques are propaganda techniques and may be applied in either a worthy or detrimental way. When applied to commercial advertising and even political campaigns, they are reluctantly accepted, but when applied to an institution like the public schools they may undermine confidence in the integrity of the school establishment.

School systems must give attention to public relations, but the best of these programs are beginning to take on the characteristics of an honest endeavor to bring the best and most adequate information possible to the public, and involve the public in setting the goals for good education.

This chapter will present ten principles of a good public information program and support each with illustrations and suggestions for their application.

Principle 1. This is the "principle of proximity."

The closer one is to something the more favorable his attitude is toward it.

In a survey I conducted of attitudes toward a new program in a large city school system, those who were most favorable were those who were the closest to it. Proximity was defined as closeness in any of its dimensions, either physical closeness or through communication.

In this survey, parents who were most favorable to the program in question were the most familiar with it. This was also true of teachers and students. Those who had a child, a friend or knew someone in the program were more favorable than those who did not. Those who had served on a committee or had their opinion sought were more favorable than those who had not. Those who had been to a meeting where the new program was discussed were more favorable than those who had not. The same was true of those who read about the program, knew someone who had been affected by it, or were otherwise associated with it, either directly or indirectly.

Even teachers whose rooms were closest to the new program centers were more favorable than those who were housed in remote parts of the building.

If an elementary principal wants a favorable attitude on the part of the parents and teachers for a new innovation, say nongradedness, he would do well to bring as many people into the discussions as possible. This could be achieved by establishing a library staff in the school about the innovation, establishing study groups, advisory committees and sponsoring speakers on the subject.

Opinion surveys are also a good device. In using opinion surveys to initiate innovations, it is better to survey opinions about *elements* of the problem and preferences about specifics, rather than head-on votes for or against the intended innovation.

Figure 8-1 shows two different approaches to opinion surveys concerning nongradedness.

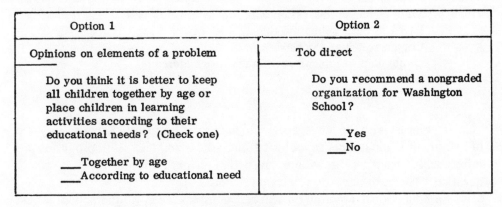

Option 1	Option 2
Opinions on elements of a problem	Too direct
Do you think it is better to keep all children together by age or place children in learning activities according to their educational needs? (Check one) ___Together by age ___According to educational need	Do you recommend a nongraded organization for Washington School? ___Yes ___No

Figure 8-1

Notice in this example that the survey which elicits honest opinions from parents on elements of a problem will help an innovator accumulate a set of specific preferences that are bite-sized, and to which most parents have sufficient information to express a preference. On the other hand, head-on direct preference statements require a judgment that parents may not have the information to make and is conclusive. It cuts off further options because it requires a final conclusion which should not be made in the early stages of a project.

Obviously, proximity is an important element in any school public information program. Schools will do well when establishing new programs to involve teachers, parents and students as much as possible. Not only will these techniques improve the programs, but they will establish in the community a group of informed, supportive people who in turn will inform others.

Principle 2. The press is a powerful media for putting across the message.

The newspaper is still the most frequent source of information about the school. This is in spite of the fact that for commercial advertising television is generally the most popular and demanding media. Newspapers get into nearly every home, and they are localized. Television, on the other hand, is national in character, with local public service time allocated to undesirable times. Local programming is either late at night, on Sunday morning, or opposite a very popular program on another channel.

Parents generally list the sources of general information about the schools in this descending order:

Newspapers[2]
Word of mouth (discussion with friends or neighbors)
PTSA or other public meetings
Conferences with teachers
Discussions of programs with their own children
Bulletins
Television and radio

In contrast with the newspaper, which is most frequently listed as a source of information about local school programs, radio and television programs are infrequently listed as the source, even though programs on the subjects in question have been aired by television or radio.

An educational reporter on a local newspaper can be the school's best friend. In the suburban community of Matson Lake, the local superintendent saw a need for a better career education program. The two high schools in the school system were academically oriented and crowded. He held discussions in the community with business and industrial leaders. Also included were a labor representative and a representative of the news media.

As discussions were held and the problem analyzed, the trend of opinion was toward the establishment of a skill center to which students could enroll from either existing high school for career education on a half-time basis. The newspaper ran regular weekly articles on the progress of the deliberations and the potential outcomes. The articles carried interviews with teachers, students, career education specialists and citizens in general.

It wasn't long before the superintendent met such comments as these on the street and in social situations: "How is your career education program coming, Joe? It sounds like a good idea." Or, "I think the establishment of a skill center is just what we need. It makes more sense than trying to remodel two crowded high schools for competing programs."

Needless to say, the newspaper was a great asset in gaining public favor for the proposal.

Principle 3. Schools should maintain a close and open relationship with the local press. This relationship can be enhanced by informing the reporters of current happenings, alerting them to interesting new developments and above all making them welcome to all board meetings.

More and more districts are adopting the open meeting policy for the

---

[2]Unpublished research by the author

conduct of school business. Some states are requiring, by legislation, open meetings of all legal bodies. Since school boards are legal bodies, their meetings are included in the state legal requirements. When an open meeting policy is adopted by a Board of Education, all meetings must be announced in advance and be open to the public. The so-called "executive sessions" are reserved for personnel and property matters. Under the open policy, the press is invited to the closed, executive sessions as a representative of the public. Their journalistic ethics determine what they may publish "in the public interest."

In Mountain View, the superintendent and Board held closed sessions. They reviewed every item in these meetings. The open meetings became pure routine. Item one on the agenda was moved by one member, seconded by the next, and then voted on, usually unanimously by the Board.

When a crisis developed over the expenditure of school funds for acquisition of property which would displace several older family homes, public opinion and newspapers came out against the proposal. All of the pertinent information had been presented in closed sessions. There was no one who knew what was going on, nor did they trust the Board. Rumors started that someone should make a big profit on the land deal. When the measure for a building fund came up for the vote of the people, it lost. People simply did not trust the Board and their judgment behind closed doors.

School administrators should develop a mutual understanding with reporters about what is in the public interest and what is not. The Board should invite them to all sessions. Obviously, the discussion of the price to be offered for a piece of property should not be publicized in advance of negotiations with the owner. It is in the public interest that the school district be in as good a bargaining position as possible. Also, it is not in the public interest to report the details of a teacher case which may come to tenure hearing. Both the rights of the teacher and of the district may be prejudiced by such disclosures. Both of these issues are in harmony with good journalistic ethical codes. The presence of reporters at closed sessions should be no threat to the conduct of good sound deliberation and policy development.

Open meetings also carry in and of themselves great public relations value. The tradition of the free press is highly valued by the American people. The press itself is a great advocate of free and open access to information. A school system that is open and above board in making information available enhances its image before the public and instills public confidence.

Principle 4. Use the correct media to fit the message. It is not advocated that media other than the press be ignored simply because of the power of the press. Radio, television bulletins and informative meetings are also important. Radio and television news programs reach a great many people. Parents, particularly, read school bulletins if the items are well chosen and well written. If a bond campaign is being conducted by the district, the message should fit the media. Spot announcements, paid for by the citizens for the bond campaign, can be very effective in bringing the message to a broad cross section of the community, while a panel discussion of the bond election scheduled for 11 a.m. Sunday morning in public service time might reach only those interested citizens who want to critically analyze the specific needs. Each should be used, but each message would be adjusted to fit the media.

Three levels of public information concerning a coming bond election follow.

LEVEL 1

A public information announcement should be done at school expense. It should be objective, giving only information needed by the public. Following is an example:

The district of Matson Lake is calling a special bond election for the vote of the people on May 30.

The purpose of the election is to provide $2,500,000 (two million, five hundred thousand dollars) in bonds to be paid over the next ten years, to be used to construct a new elementary school and make capital improvements on existing structures.

The Board of Education has determined the need for construction to avoid double shifting in two elementary schools. Older buildings are inadequate to meet modern educational and safety standards.

LEVEL 2

Paid Radio or Television Spot Announcement

We urge you vote "yes" on the school bond levy on May 30. Help us maintain our present high educational standards and avoid undesirable double shifting in our schools. Our children deserve a better break in Matson Lake.

Vote *Yes* on May 30.

Paid for by the Good Schools Committee.

LEVEL 3

Television Forum Discussion

The superintendent and the chairman of the Good Schools Committee are interviewed by the local radio and television educational reporter.

Announcer: Mr. Superintendent, why do the schools need another $2,500,000 at this time?

Superintendent: The simple reason is that we have very old buildings in our school system, all built more than 40 years ago, and our population is growing at the rate of 90 children (3 classrooms) per year.

Announcer: Mrs. Smith, you are the chairman of the Good Schools Committee. What does your group feel about this bond election?
Mrs. Smith: We are for it. We have studied the issue carefully and we think this amount is a modest sum to spend to assure that our children will continue to have an adequate education in Matson Lake.

Principle 5. Expend public funds for public information prudently.

Since bond issues have been mentioned, a fuller discussion of the schools' roles in campaigns is appropriate here. Any district should consult legal authorities before expending public funds on any campaign literature. Usually courts have held that public funds can be used to provide information about the election and the needs for the funds. It cannot be used, however, for public campaigns or advertising. This must be done with private political funds. The line is fine and administrators and Boards must exercise careful judgment in the use of money to conduct bond campaigns.

Otherwise, it appears to be perfectly legal to use school funds, personnel and duplicating services to prepare and distribute public information material about schools. This is part of the obligation of a school district and should be provided for.

The example in Level I generally would meet the criteria for a public information announcement. It is factual and objective. It is the kind of information that voters must have in order to vote intelligently, and it should be paid for from public funds.

Level 2, however, is pure campaigning. Public funds of any kind should not be used for this kind of announcement. also, almost any paper, radio or television station which carried such a spot announcement would have to charge for it as a political announcement.

The Level 3 example is a discussion. Such programs are properly public service programs and should be carried as part of the obligation of stations under their FCC licensing.

Principle 6. Talk to the public in plain language.

Educators, like other professionals, adopt a technical language as a short cut to effective communication within the profession. Unlike some other professions, however, educators tend to be imprecise in their use of technical language. The word "curriculum" might mean the course of study in one case, the teaching techniques applied in a particular school in another case, or still in other cases the behavioral changes effected in a student through his total school experiences. Educators have a tendency to use technical terms among themselves and with the public without sufficient interpretation. In the case of the word "curriculum," in many instances a clearer message can be transmitted if more precise and understandable terms such as "course of study," "instructional program," "teaching methods," or something equally understandable are used.

One report in an educational journal listed 29 new terms which came into common use in educational circles within the two years of 1968-1970. These were called "educationese," and were defined for educators, so that they could communicate among themselves. The terms included such usages as "differentiated staffing," "behavior modification," "bilingual education," "continuous progress," and "parochiaid," to name but a few of the most common. If it was necessary to define these for professionals, think of how confused the general public must feel when such terms are used with them indiscriminately.

Here are some alternative terms that can make things clear to the public.

TECHNICAL	PLAIN ENGLISH
Curriculum	Teaching program or instructional program
Differentiated staffing	More efficient use of teachers
Behavior modification	Application of modern psychological principles to help children learn better
Bilingual education	Teaching in two languages, the child's first language and English
Continuous progress	Placing children in classes according to their progress by subject
Parochiaid	Providing tax money for parochial schools

These illustrations do not mean that no technical terms should be used; but when they are used, at least a definition of the term should be given to assure understanding.

Principle 7. Explain innovations before they are introduced.

Most good school systems in this country are trying one or more innovative practices at any given time because good schools are those that are responsive to the needs of students and to the ideas of creative teachers. Teachers who are involved in such programs usually grow in their perceptions and skills. An innovative school is a beehive of activity. Professionals, students and involved parents alike are communicating more effectively and coordinating their efforts. Such schools are real centers for growth, and children are the benefactors.

It is too bad that innovations often fail because of lack of adequate understanding on the part of parents about what is happening. Some parents are very concerned when they hear of unfamiliar practices going on in school. "What do you mean you have three teachers in your room?" Or, "You mean to say you don't have homework anymore? I never heard of such a thing. It's ridiculous!"

Parents cannot be expected to see the point if it is never explained to them. A simple technique used by one school system was to prepare a question-and-answer bulletin regarding a new nongraded program. They invited a group of parents to sit in with the teachers and assist them in explaining their new program to other parents by answering the questions which were of most concern.

Such questions as the following were listed:

What is a nongraded elementary school?
How is the school organized?
What are the advantages to students of this organization?
How is the child placed in the program?
How are we sure that the placement is correct?
What is used to determine when a child is to be removed or advanced
in the program?

A bulletin was prepared listing these questions separately and answered sequentially, as in the following examples:

Question: What is a nongraded elementary school?
Answer: A nongraded elementary school is one which permits each child to progress systematically in his learning activities without the restriction of being in a particular grade.

Question: How is the school organized?
Answer: The school is organized by age groups for the general homeroom activities, but children leave their homeroom to study their lessons according to their needs. For example, some very advanced six-year-olds will be taking reading instruction with some older children and some eight-year-olds will be doing some of their work with younger children.

Question: What are the advantages to students of this organization?
Answer: Each child can progress at his own rate and can work with others at the same level of achievement. Teachers can concentrate on the needs of children with similar needs, etc.

This is only one illustration of a simple and straightforward method of communication through the use of a bulletin. It is not intended to be the only approach. The use of parents, however, in generating questions and concerns to be answered is by far the most effective way of planning a bulletin for public information about new and innovative programs being introduced.

Principle 8. View report cards as a public information media.

As much controversy centers around the report card as any other form of message to school patrons. It is truly a public information device for the following reasons:

1. It gets into the home of every parent.
2. It contains information about the program of studies for every child.
3. It reflects the instructional philosophy of the school system through what is reported.
4. It provides the parents with a record of the continuous educational growth of their child.
5. It is one of the most personalized devices for informing the parents of what the school is doing for their child.

Report cards with letter grades are still used by about 80 percent of the teachers. The tendency for deviation from letter grades is more prevalent and most often acceptable to parents at the primary grade level than at the upper or high school level.

Yet even at the primary levels parents want and need a good interpretation of the educational objectives. Instead of listing "uses scissors well," say "is developing small muscle coordination." In this manner schools can avoid looking ridiculous. For instance, one parent made the comment to friends that his little girl failed cutting in kindergarten because she didn't use scissors well. Imagine the effect this had on the child as well as the school image.

Schools which deviate their student reporting systems should accompany such efforts by parent study groups and a considerable effort to interpret the new reporting system. As the new system becomes established, schools sometimes forget to continue the interpretation, as new parents progress through the system with their children. Consequently, reporting practices come under periodic attack from parent groups if such reporting systems deviate too far from the usual.

In designing reporting systems, every effort should be made to make them real vehicles for communication. Few school systems believe in absolute comparisons among children without regard to a child's ability to achieve in the academic areas. Some compromise must be reached so that parents can understand what their child is achieving and how satisfactory this achievement is according to reasonable expectations.

Various alternatives to traditional grades on report cards have been tried and are meeting with intermittent success. These range from parent-teacher conferences and simple written messages on report cards with blank spaces, to various devices for using symbols for both "working to ability" and "achievement."

No one device of reporting is ever completely successful. Usually a combination of communication systems is best.

It is not the purpose here to present a complete discussion of reporting systems; rather this discussion is to call attention to the consideration of reporting practices in the public information program of the school.

When tampering with the reporting practices it is recommended that changes be made progressively—a little at a time instead of broad, sweeping changes all at once. This takes the parents from the known to the unknown in progressive steps. Remember that parents, like all people are most threatened by abrupt departure from expectations.

> Principle 9. Homework should not disrupt family life, but should enhance school-home cooperation.

Homework often becomes a negative influence on public understanding and acceptance of the school program.

Most parents who become uptight about homework complain first to friends and neighbors and then to the principal. The last to know may be the teacher. Parents who have discussed homework in study groups most generally mention the following:

1. Assignments which appear to have little value for the time spent—hours spent in making elaborate notebooks.
2. Vague instructions—directions that are unclear and imprecise.
3. Assignments which make demands on the parents—a requirement that every child in the first grade take a trip to the zoo or collect so many specimens of sea life.
4. Unchecked homework—homework that is thoroughly prepared but not graded by the teacher.
5. Mechanical tasks—dull memorization tasks or repetitious drill.
6. Piling up of assignments among teachers—four teachers giving heavy assignments at the same time.
7. Assignments over holiday periods—a theme to be written over the Thanksgiving vacation.
8. Purpose not clear—assignments to research questions which do not fit into a reasonable whole.

Parents do approve of homework which children understand and see the reason for. They also like assignments which give the children a choice and which truly supplement the work being done at school. Individualized home study programs can also be successful for those children who have special interests or need special work.

Principle 10. Children are the ambassadors who explain the school to the parents and the public.

Children who are involved and enthusiastic about their school programs, and who feel they are making real progress, are the best public relations agents a school can have. This implies that schools should help every child establish his own learning goals, participate in planning how to reach those goals and help in the evaluation of his own progress.

Many good teachers work with students as much on the learning process as on the content. They use diagnostic techniques to help each child understand his particular needs. They help students set their own learning goals and reduce these goals to "my learning objectives," "my learning activities" and assessment of "how well I did and how I know I did well."

Children who understand this much about their learning not only do better in school, but they also make good ambassadors for the schools.

These ten principles have several dimensions. One dimension is involvement. Those who are involved usually support the program. Another dimension is use of media. The vehicle for communication should fit the message. A third dimension is language. The plainer the language, the clearer the message becomes.

The final dimension is school procedure. These procedural ways of doing things in and of themselves carry a message, and should be considered important means of communication.

A public information program, with the ultimate goal of having an informed and supportive public, cannot be isolated from the general operation of the school. Schools that show concern for the students and have procedures that are logical and systematic create a holistic pattern which in and of itself transmits a powerful message.

In the final analysis, excellence wins out! Good schools are in and of themselves the best public relations devices there are. But good schools result from the things that build public confidence in the schools. This book speaks of good schools. It advocates careful analysis of need, goal setting, techniques for planning, means of involving the people in decision making, ways to build staff competencies, and responsible reporting. All of these are necessary ingredients of a good school system and result in something worth reporting. The ten principles presented in this chapter are suggested as a checklist against which schools can mind the details. However, the school must first be adequate. Second, they should use the techniques necessary to make this adequacy or excellence known to the public.

SUMMARY

The general public has a high level of awareness of the importance of good education, but they have little concept of the cause and effect of good education. On the one hand, they will favor small classes; however, they will not translate this need into the need for more tax dollars.

Early school public relations programs are giving way to better public information programs. The main goal of these public information programs is to provide the public with accurate information of all aspects of the schools and their needs. They differ from public relations programs in that their main purpose is to "inform," not to "sell" the school programs.

The ten principles of good public information are a combination of effective communications devices and processes for involving the public in decision processes whenever possible.

These ten principles are:

1. The principle of proximity. The closer a person is to a program (either physical closeness or involvement), the more favorable that person becomes toward it.
2. The press is the most powerful medium in a public information program. Despite the glamor of television, radio and other media, the press (newspapers) is still the major source of accurate information about the schools.
3. An open door policy with the press is important. Open Board meetings and frank discussions of school problems with representatives of the press build trust in the schools on the part of the whole community.
4. The use of the correct media is important. Brochures, television, public meetings all have their place, but should be used for different purposes.
5. Expend public funds for public information prudently. Use of school funds to provide information to the public is a legitimate expenditure. Use of such funds to "promote" a new tax base might be an illegal use of public funds.
6. Talk in plain language. Educators tend to use either technical terms or highly imprecise language in describing their programs. These should be reduced to plain talk understandable by all.
7. Explain innovations before they are introduced. If new and unusual approaches are used, explain them and their purposes to the public beforehand.

8. Report cards are a public information device. The most consistent information system for parents is the report card. It should be designed to explain the school to the parents.
9. Homework should not disrupt family life, but should enhance school-home cooperation. Parents do approve homework if they see it as having an educational purpose.
10. Children are the ambassadors. Children who are happy in school and feel they are learning are the best public relations devices a school could have.

9

How to Decentralize the Decision
Structures with Alternative School
Organizational Plans

WAYS TO ASSURE SUCCESS IN
DECENTRALIZED DECISION PROCESSES

When there was only one teacher in a school, there was no need for an administrative organizational plan. It requires two or more people working together for a common purpose to have an organization. As more teachers are added, the organization becomes more complex, and role definitions must become more precise. The larger the organization becomes, the more complex it must be, and the more influence the organization has upon the behavior of its own members.

In a very large school, for example, there may be an attendance secretary who does nothing but keep the records of attendance, while in a smaller school this task may be done casually in a few minutes per day by a teacher, a general secretary or the principal. Expectations, then, in these two different sized organizations, are very different, and the member of the larger organization has a much more controlled, restricted and specialized role than a person in a smaller school.

During each decade since 1920, much attention was given to different aspects of school organization. As a result of this attention we saw the development of various plans for the delivery of educational services; the departmentalization of elementary and secondary schools alike; and the development of junior high schools and various other combinations, such as 8-4, 6-3-3, 6-6, and now the 4-4-4 or middle school plan.

All of these organizational plans were arrangments for grouping students into the most teachable groups, in an effort to gain more efficiency.

Until about 1955 most of the organizational plans were highly centralized vith hierarchical authority. Especially in the largest districts, the central office was all powerful. Decisions rested mainly at this level, with the intermediate administrators and teachers being left with little autonomy. Their main functions were to *enforce* rules, *follow* procedures and *use* the established lines of communication. Textbooks, courses of study and supplies were standardized, sometimes at the state level. The regulatory function of school administrative offices were emphasized—often to the degree that school districts or single schools were inspected, rated and classified as "standard," "nonstandard" or perhaps "superior."

Recently, we have seen a swing away from the highly centralized authority and regulatory function of administration toward decentralization of authority. This swing was in response to the need for meeting new concerns for plurality, responsiveness to local needs and the need for creativity in the solution of school problems. Large schools were trying to become small in their organizational structure.

Federal legislation and funding policies contributed to the acceleration of the change toward less standardization. The federal funds were provided for disadvantaged children, for head start programs and for various creative endeavors. The efforts were invariably aimed at the school unit or a special population within a school, rather than at a district as a whole. Thus, they promoted localization of the decision processes.

During the last two decades this swing was away from centralized, regulatory and standardization efforts toward local autonomy, with fewer standards and fewer requirements being handed down from the central office. We sometimes are seeing, within a single school district, some schools which have early childhood and kindergarten programs while others do not; schools using different basic textbooks; and even schools with different attendance requirements.

The decentralization of school management has brought with it several sets of problems. In this chapter, these problems will be identified and some techniques will be suggested to help overcome them.

THE NEED FOR A SYSTEM OF SANCTION

All responsible leadership must be responsible *to* someone. In the case of the superintendent, the responsibility is to the Board of Education. The Board of Education is responsible to the electorate. Principals have traditionally been responsible to the superintendent, teachers to principals, etc.

Those who had to take action followed policies and procedures generated for them by the group to which they were responsible. If they deviated from the hierarchical arrangement, it was necessary to get permission or *sanction* for their actions.

Sanction was important for several reasons. It gave assurance of mutual support. The agreement between a teacher and the administrator showed agreement that the action was reasonable and well thought out. Each role player, in turn, played his role in sanctioning the procedures of others as reasonable and responsible.

With decentralization, these traditional roles were interrupted and became less definite. The decentralized organization put intermediate leadership into a role requiring more independence, which supposedly made it more responsive to local needs. Who was to determine these needs and sanction the action was not very clear in a decentralized organization.

Jim Carter was the principal of the city's technical high school. He wanted to make it the best technical school in the state, and therefore he wanted to attract only students who were interested in engineering and who had a good background in reading and mathematics. He advocated the establishment of entrance requirements for his high school. Certainly this action required sanction on the part of the superintendent and the Board of Education, because each of these levels would be highly affected by the action Jim took. Also, other high schools would be affected, as well as the local trade associations which had helped build pre-apprentice trade programs into the school.

In the case of Jim Carter, he needed either the sanction of the Board and superintendent or some other group.

One response to this need for sanction in decentralized organizations has been the establishment of localized advisory groups. These groups are established as advisory or policy review groups for the decentralized activities. They are usually appointed by the legal authority of the district, the school board. They themselves must report and receive sanction for their activities, as does any other group.

Jim, under this system, made his recommendation to his school advisory committee, which represented the parents, professional engineers and the trade groups. They were able to hold the necessary hearings, interpret points of view and support some of Jim's recommendations to the legal authority. In Jim's case his recommendation was greatly modified by this process. There was agreement that pre-engineering was important but that other technical and trade programs were also important. When the recommendation went to the Board that more careful counseling be provided for those who entered the technical school, it could be approved because it had received the sanction of the groups most affected.

Sanction is essential because:

1. It assures support of those who share responsibility for the decision.
2. It provides for careful preparation and study of changes before they are made, and thus prevents hasty and ill-considered action.
3. It gives clear authorization to the administrator to move ahead.

In the case of decentralized organization, some of the sanctioning roles must be delegated to local advisory committees.

THE DELEGATION OF AUTHORITY

Some efforts to decentralize have not resulted in real delegation of authority to go with responsibility. The expectation from above is still toward regulatory function, and the ability to say "no," but seldom "yes," is stressed.

Let's take the example of a local school faculty which determines that one way to improve primary reading programs would be to stagger attendance patterns of primary children, with some children arriving early, say at 8:30 a.m. The next group would come at 10:30 a.m. The two groups would overlap for the hours in the middle of the day. The late arriving group would then stay two hours after the early group departed. This arrangement would assure a teacher of a small group at both ends of the day for intensive instruction. During the time when both groups were present, teachers would carry on activities suitable for the larger groups.

Does the decentralized organization carry with it the authority to make such changes in the school schedule? Probably not, unless specific authority has been delegated to change school attendance hours. The regulatory function of intermediate administrators has, in the past, been to see that rules were followed. Therefore, their traditional roles were to say, "No, you cannot change school attendance hours." They usually did not have authority to approve such a deviation, only to enforce the present rules.

This example could be multiplied many times over. How much authority will the decentralized administrators have over staffing patterns, buying supplies, changing courses of study, excusing children from regular attendance patterns and the management of school buildings?

Plans for decentralizing administration patterns usually have not been accompanied by adequate plans for delegating authority. The whole idea is to make the decentralized unit more responsive. Therefore, as much authority as reasonable must be delegated to as low a level as possible. Otherwise, decentralization will not and cannot achieve its purposes. Rather, it becomes simply another device for relieving pressure on the central administration by spreading out the accountability for the conduct of the schools—without the equivalent delegation of authority to go with it.

Decentralized decision-making processes require specific, often legal action to appropriately delegate authority to local levels. The state law may say that "school attendance hours shall be fixed by local school boards." "The Board simply cannot delegate something which the law specifically fixes with them. In the case cited, then, the desired change of attendance hours in the local schools can only be recommended. The final decision cannot be truly delegated unless the law is changed. The Board can, on the other hand, pass a resolution establishing broad parameters for attendance hours and delegate within those parameters, but they cannot truly delegate authority which is theirs by law.

The need, then, in a decentralized system is to redraw whole sets of policies spelling out clearly those decisions which can truly be delegated.

Delegated authority requires:

1. Consideration for the legal fixing of responsibility: those responsibilities fixed by law cannot be delegated to others.
2. Establishment of parameters: spelling out of parameters within which decisions can be delegated is important.
3. Establishment of whole new sets of policies and procedures: these must spell out the degree of delegation to intermediate administrators and their advisory boards.

PROVISION FOR RESPONSIVENESS TO LOCAL NEEDS

Autonomy and self-direction are attractive concepts. They have sometimes been misinterpreted as *license*. In one school district, three principals reacted differently to the new decentralized plans. One high school principal had always wanted a better athletic department. He immediately relieved his head coach of teaching duties, thus increasing other teachers' teaching loads. He authorized the purchase of a new electric scoreboard, using almost all available funds from the equipment budget. This was popular with the Dad's club and the athletic department, but not so popular with the teachers who had to take on heavier teaching loads and give up anticipated teaching equipment.

Another principal had always wanted to do something for the slow learners. He established a "business English" class for them so that they wouldn't have to study the regular course of study. He also put more of them into drama, home economics and industrial arts. These moves were popular with the academic teachers, but not with the teachers of the subjects affected by the transfers. These teachers saw the moves as making their classes dumping groups, thus losing status for the better students and preventing them from teaching effectively in their major field of preparation. They in fact had to design new curricula for the slow learners, many of whom were no more interested in these courses than the previous academic ones.

The third principal knew that the population in his high school had changed markedly over the past five years. The school had formerly served an upper middle income group and had emphasized academic preparation for college. Now, fewer than 50 percent of the students went to college. He established a faculty senate to assess the needs as they saw them. He also organized a student advisory group and a parent advisory group to conduct a needs assessment and initiate planning to diversify the program and make it more responsive to the needs of the present population.

His response was not as rapid as principals one and two, but it held much more promise of success.

Being responsive to local needs is much more complex than simply doing what "I've always wanted to be free to do."

It puts all of the requirements of responsible program analysis and systematic planning, which had formerly rested in the central office, at the local level. There is no room for license in such an arrangement, but there is the requirement of responsible leadership.

Responsiveness to local need:

1. Requires all the careful planning at the local level that was formerly done at the district level.
2. Should not be confused with *license*, which implies unrestrained liberty of action on the part of the administrator.
3. Should be based upon carefully analyzed needs of the local situation.

DECENTRALIZED CONTROL OF RESOURCES

One of the most knotty problems to overcome in decentralizing administrative procedures is that of allocating resources. Most highly centralized administrative arrangements allocate resources according to some formula. These formulas usually cover: (1) staff allocation—so many teachers for a given number of students, (2) materials allocations—so many books (often centrally selected) per student, (3) supply allocations—so much money per pupil, and (4) central purchasing—a requisitioning procedure from central storerooms.

Principals have traditionally fought very hard to maintain a high level of allocation for their schools. Some have been more successful in getting a great many things and extra teachers for their schools, while others have not done so well. And still more principals pride themselves on running economical schools.

Anytime you deviate from a set formula, you begin to have trouble. Yet if schools are to be individualized and able to respond to local needs, the formulas must be deviated from.

"Why," might you ask, "should some schools spend almost twice as much as others to educate a child? Is this fair? "The answer is, "It might be fair and it might not, depending upon the educational needs of the children."

American educators have long since departed from the concept that equal educational expenditure means equal educational opportunity. This is particularly notable in the case of physically or mentally handicapped children, whose programs may be two or three times as expensive as those for children in the normal range.

The principle of equal educational opportunity according to need has been well accepted by both educators and the public. The manner of dividing the resources equitably, however, has never been generally accepted.

Formulas are helpful and should be maintained for the general program. Then there must be ways to "add on" for special needs. These special, more costly programs are generally recognized as:

1. Programs for the handicapped.
2. Programs for disadvantaged "poor," children who have fewer rich learning opportunities in the home.
3. Remedial programs.
4. Technical, vocational or career programs.
5. Innovative and other experimental programs.

Other considerations must be made for small schools, schools which are new, or schools which have other unusual circumstances.

An effective and equitable way to allocate resources to local educational units is to:

1. Use the basic formula for the general program of the school.
2. Make a "small school" or "new school" correction.
3. Add on other allocations for the special program needs as enumerated.

The add-on's should be according to program needs—not formula, and usually are justified by application of PPBS analysis techniques.

AVOIDING DUPLICATION OF EFFORT

One of the advantages of a big organization is that it can afford a high degree of specialization. Specialization was carried to such an extent in some school systems that there was not room for individualization. That is, all books were approved by a specialist, all testing was done by a testing expert, and all teacher assignments were made by the personnel department. At one time in the history of American education, one could have gone into some city school systems where the superintendent could have said with pride, "It is now 10 a.m., and I can tell you exactly what every third grader in the district is studying and what page in the textbook his lesson will be on today."

This was carrying specialization and centralization to a ridiculous extreme. Fortunately, such a tendency in the late 1920's and early '30's was short lived. Such practices gave specialization a bad name.

The tendency to decentralize has carried with it, however, some potential for overdoing the elimination of specialists. It was popular during the 1960's to eliminate central office staffs of specialists. Whole staffs of supervisors were reassigned or dismissed, leaving the schools "autonomous"to conduct their own programs.

Teachers in special areas such as music, kindergarten, science and home economics soon found that their programs suffered through lack of the resource help formerly supplied by a specialist. Systematic processes for evaluating and obtaining instructional materials were interrupted. Book salesmen began calling on individual schools or individual teachers in an effort to sell their wares. Questions from parents had to be channeled to the local level. Teachers had to be released from classroom duties to answer questions of new teachers, to prepare lists of materials, and to do a myriad of other things that had formerly been done by central office specialists.

The tendency is for each new autonomous unit of the organization to fill the gap by replacing central specialists with local specialists. This results in a heavy duplication of efforts. Balance is needed. Decisions must be made as to which specialists to retain and how to share the use of specialists among the local units.

The most flexible approach to shared utilization of services is to establish procedures for "shared services." Small rural schools have done this for years by joining together to obtain the services of specialists which they could not individually afford. States have tended to break the regions down into intermediate districts, replacing county offices to provide special services.

Obviously, districts that decentralize still need the services of specialists. Which specialists and how much authority they will have must be negotiated. Those that can be afforded and maintained at the local administrative levels should be there. Those that are needed across administrative units should be provided in centers governed by a council of representatives from the affected users of the service. Such cooperative arrangements will lessen the tendencies for wasteful duplication.

The maintenance of specialists in a decentralized system is difficult. It requires:

1. The selection of only a few specialists at the local administrative unit.
2. The establishment of shared service centers for specialists who cannot be afforded at the local unit level.

3. The establishment of a governance procedure for the service center to assure the responsiveness of the specialists to the needs of local administrative units.

THE NEED FOR A SYSTEM OF
BUDGET MANAGEMENT INFORMATION

A highly centralized school operation requires very simple budget management for information systems. The business manager has the budget. He processes all expenditure requests and has the account balances before him at all times. When an account has been exhausted, he simply cuts off expenditures or initiates a budget transfer.

If a district is to have decentralized decision making and local control, this kind of management information must be available to the local decision makers.

An efficient management information system for modern day decision making requires a computerized reporting system, preferably individualized to the needs of the particular manager. Computer budget printouts show the original budget, the expenditures made against it during the last month, and the balance remaining. The backup sheets for the monthly expenditures should show the specific amount paid and to whom. These are the minimum requirements of an adequate management information system. More elaborate systems can be designed to carry more and more categories of information and complex analysis summaries. But these probably are not advisable for the usual school system.

The information system must be tailored to the needs of the decision makers. If the local principal has control of the supply budget only, then this is the only information he needs. If on the other hand he has responsibility for staffing costs, equipment purchase, telephone costs and custodial costs, he must also receive this information.

Mary Taylor was accountable for the supply budget for her school. When she received the November printout, she noticed that a $2,000 charge had been made for the month. She quickly looked at the backup sheet for her printout. There was an item titled "distribution of annual supply handling costs." This told her that the costs of packing and shipping supplies to her school were "distributed" arbitrarily to schools within the district. Being a new principal, she immediately called the business manager of the district. He was able to interpret the basis for such a charge and to give her the detailed information she needed for verifying the correctness of the assessment. If it was incorrect, she would have been able to request a correction. Without backup information including lists of charges, she would have had no way of knowing what specific charges had been made to her accounts.

Decentralization has been feasible with the introduction of computerized information feedback. Most school systems, especially large ones, now have computerized management information services available to them. This service, for most moderate or small-sized districts is usually a shared service through some intermediate or cooperative service agency.

Such information services are a necessity if decision making is to be decentralized.

The requirements are that:

1. The responsible administrator must receive periodic budget management information in the areas for which he is responsible.
2. The management information should minimally include the originial budget, recent expenditures and funds remaining.
3. Backup sheets for expenditures must enumerate the specific items listed as expenditures.

This kind of information is feasible through the use of computerized systems.

ACCOUNTABILITY SYSTEMS

Local autonomy carries with it the necessity of redefining the accountability system. With the appointment of local advisory groups of intermediate administrative coordinators, old lines of reporting are broken down and must be replaced by new understandings.

A few years back some large cities established local advisory boards. Some of the first proposals of the committees were to fire the principal or replace some teachers. The roles of the advisory groups had obviously not been defined and their understanding of the system of accountability was erroneous. Yet if new decision groups are to be introduced, and if staff is maintained to help carry out the programs, then accountability to the group is inferred.

This brings us to the categories of legal versus informal accountability. The legal accountability is logically through the hierarchical arrangements of the school system. There is informal responsibility to others, however.

This level of accountability can usually be handled through an efficient reporting system. Intermediate and advisory groups legitimately can and should expect response to their advice and requests. They have a right to have them systematically analyzed, studied and evaluated.

In Canyonbrook, a local advisory committee became concerned about equal opportunities for girls. They looked at the recreational program and found that three-fourths of the expenditures for intramural programs, and virtually all the athletic funds, were allocated to boys' activities. They passed a resolution to the effect that girls should have equal access to funded recreational activities and at least some opportunities to participate in competitive sports. The regional administrator was accountable to the advisory group for doing his best to implement their recommendation or influencing them to modify it. He reported to the advisory group his analysis of the programs and the alternatives available for modifying present programs. The advisory group was then able to make specific recommendations for the introduction of girls' intramural activities and such other sports as volleyball, girls basketball, and individual sports in which girls could participate. These would cost more money.

A decision was reached to request such funds in next year's budget, but if they were not forthcoming, to modify the boys' program to meet the needs of girls.

The administrator was equally accountable to this group and to his former hierarchical bosses in the traditional line of command.

Accountability under decentralized systems requires dual responsibility.

1. The administrator must respond to the recommendations of the local advisory group.
2. He must advise them of alternative ways of achieving their goals.
3. He must explain these recommendations to the hierarchical, legal authorities.
4. He must report back to the local groups the decisions regarding their recommendations.

THE COORDINATION OF PLANNING EFFORTS

Of all functions consistently carried on in a school district, systematic planning has probably been neglected most. This is understandable. School systems are geared to program operation, not planning. The teachers are hired, children arrive and schools must go into daily operation. This is the highest priority. Consequently, school districts gear their resources to maintaining the school system.

Few resources remain for the establishment and maintenance of an adequate planning system. Therefore, school systems are often thrown into a responsive mode rather than a leadership role. They are so busy responding to needs and emergencies, that little time and money are left over for adequate planning.

If school systems are to establish and maintain a good planning system, they must deliberately set aside resources (time, money and people) to do the planning.

Although planning should be carried on at every level in the district, there should be a centralized planning effort. This can be, for large districts, through a department with specialists, or through shared responsibility in smaller districts.

The minimum elements of a planning system would require:

1. A system and responsibility for reviewing and analyzing data: test results, attendance patterns, potential resources, expenditure patterns and population trends.
2. A system and responsibility for the identification of needs and projection of goals.
3. A system and responsibility for the projection of alternatives and costs of goals for the district (both educational goals and institutional goals). Institutional goals are those that are responsive to the needs of the institution as a whole.
4. A system and responsibility for analyzing and selecting feasible and cost-effective alternatives.
5. Finally, there must be an evaluation system for gathering data about the effectiveness of the alternatives which were selected and put into effect.

The reader will readily recognize these essentials as the steps advocated by PPBS systems. The steps defined for PPBS are minimum for any planning effort.

THE COORDINATION OF PERSONNEL TRAINING EFFORTS

Once a program is established in a school system, it must be maintained. Many school systems buy new equipment or adopt new procedures without giving adequate attention to installation and maintenance of the program. No industry would do this. Any time new machinery and production processes are installed, the personnel who will operate the system are trained, provided with supervision, and new employees are adequately trained before they begin operation. School systems, on the other hand, often expect new programs to install themselves and maintain themselves without providing time and money for those purposes.

If you don't believe this is true, just look around at the number of schools that have expensive language laboratories and coordinated multimedia teaching resources inadequately used or not used at all.

The plea here is for a planned resource allocation for personnel training to accompany new programs.

The minimum requirements of such a program would include four aspects of personnel training:

1. *Orientation to the new programs or media.* If it is a new instructional device, demonstrations and hands-on training must be provided. If it is a new

mathematics adaptation, the program should include explanations of the philosophy of the system, explanation of the materials and how they were engineered to be used, and actual demonstration of how to use the processes.

2. *Consultation as the personnel begin to use the new program or media.* This is a step most often left out. Personnel, no matter how well trained initially, always run into difficulty in using new materials and new approaches. They should have available to them someone who can answer their questions, give additional information, and exchange information among the users as to how to overcome unforeseen difficulties.

3. *Orientation of new personnel.* Many districts do provide for meetings of the initial personnel for new programs, but they forget that a new person coming in the second or third year of the program needs the same training and assistance provided the original group.

4. *Evaluation and feedback services.* Almost any new system requires adjustments as it is put into operation. Questionnaires, interviews, and other data-gathering processes must be employed to identify these trouble spots. These data, with suggestions, should be provided the users of the program. It is part of the inservice maintenance effort for the program.

In decentralized districts, all of these activities should be coordinated and shared across administrative areas. Parallel efforts can sometimes be provided among the administrative units. Shared services should be arranged whenever more efficiency can be attained.

SUMMARY

The recent efforts to improve the effectiveness of school district organizations have resulted in decentralized and somewhat autonomous administrative units. Sometimes these units are area districts or individual schools. This is an effort to make the local units more "effective," not necessarily more "efficient."

Many problems come to the fore when decision structures are broken down into autonomous units. The local or intermediate administrative unit becomes a leader and a decision maker instead of a regulator. In other words, he must take the initiative, do the planning, and provide the leadership in working out policies and procedures at the unit level. This is instead of his former regulatory role of enforcing policies and procedures prepared by a higher authority.

Sometimes intermediate administrators mistake their new roles for license, instead of a new and more intense degree of responsibility and accountability. In order to operate effectively and efficiently in such a system, the following needs were discussed in this chapter.

1. *The need for a system of sanction*

Sanction is important because it provides each administrator assurance of the necessary information to share in the accountability system. Who is to provide the sanction for plans and programs designed by the local or inter-mediate administrative units? This is a problem that must be addressed if a decentralized plan is to be successful. Sanction is a shared responsibility of the hierarchical, legal authority as well as local advisory groups.

2. *The delegation of authority*

Many administrators are quick to delegate the responsibility of running schools to a person closer to the operational units. This is not always accom-panied by the like amount of authority to go with the responsibility. Responsi-bility is always accompanied by authority. Without authority to act, an ad-ministrator cannot be held accountable. Careful definitions of areas of authority must accompany any new scheme for passing on responsibility. Only those decisions that are not legally fixed can be delegated to lower authority.

3. *Provision for responsiveness to local needs*

Since the only reason for decentralizing decision making is to improve effectiveness, the local units must be more responsive to local needs. This requires the kind of needs assessments and program planning at the local level that was formerly done at the central level.

4. *Decentralized control of resources*

Delegation of responsibility and authority doesn't mean a thing unless the control of resources goes along with it. Usually, this is the last thing given to local administrators. This chapter recommends allocation of funds according to a formula for the general program, with "add-on's" for special needs or programs justified at the local level. This justification should follow PPBS analysis processes.

5. *Avoiding duplication of efforts*

One of the advantages of centralized control of school programs was that there could be a large number of specialists: supervisors, engineers, psychologists, etc. The tendency is for local administrators to want to build complete staffs in their own areas. The duplication of efforts in these "paral-lel" systems can be avoided by the establishment of shared services which are coordinated, controlled and supported jointly across local units.

6. *The need for a system of budget management information*

The introduction of administrative use of the computers has made decen-tralized administration and decision making feasible. An adequate system of expenditure reporting, with appropriate backup sheets of specific charges, can be supplied monthly to each administrative unit. This is necessary if decen-tralized control of resources is to be achieved.

7. *Accountability systems*

Central administration provides for accountability right up the hierarchical ladder. With decentralized control, the local administrator must be accountable to the local unit which he serves, as well as to the legal authority. A minimum accountability to the local unit would be a systematic reporting system to local advisory groups, with a log of action taken and reasons for no action, on all recommendations received.

8. *The need for coordinated planning efforts*

School systems find it difficult to plan adequately. This is because of the high priority given to the daily operation of the school system. Consequently, school systems often find all of their time and effort being taken up in responding rather than leading in the area of planning.

Coordinated local district-wide planning should follow the four basic steps advocated by PPBS as a guide, whether or not the complete system is utilized.

9. *Coordination of personnel training efforts*

Many programs fail, regardless of the good intentions of people, simply because too little attention is given to the needs for good personnel training programs for the installation and maintenance of new programs. No modern industry would neglect this item. A minimum training program includes: (1) initial training, (2) consultation, (3) orientation of new personnel and (4) an evaluation-feedback system.

Localization of decision processes has much to recommend it as a potential for more effective educational programs. Much attention must be given to safeguarding the efficiency lost from the former centralized systems. The opportunities and responsibilities of local or intermediate administrators are greatly increased.

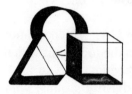

10

Responsibility—Using a Decision Matrix Delegation Flow to Fix Responsibility[1]

The lack of a clear decision-sharing process promotes suspicion and rumor. When people do not know what is going on they are prey to rumors and discontent. They develop a feeling of despair when complex situations arise over which they feel they have no control.

As a psychologist puts it:

"One of the favorite ways people explain the action of others is in terms of the other person's motivation. As people become more isolated from each other and have access to less and less information in common, the tendency increases to interpret actions as evidence of plots and counterplots, political maneuvers, etc. If the result of a lack of coordination is believed deliberately intended, then, obviously, somebody is suspected of having harmful or destructive intentions. An emphasis on 'going through channels' thus results in an increase of distrust and suspicion which further increases the isolation and problems of coordination."[2]

This chapter offers a highly effective technique for resolving problems of misunderstanding of who has what responsibility for what decisions. The tech-

---

[1]The processes discussed in this chapter were originally presented in an article in *Educational Leadership*, Hamilton, Norman K., "The Decision Making Structure of a School System," Volume 29, Number 8, May 1972.

[2]John L. Wallen, *Charting the Decision Making Structure of an Organization*, Program Report: Improving Teaching Competencies Program. Northwest Regional Educational Laboratory, Portland, Oregon 1971, p. 2.

nique is that of preparing a decision matrix (or chart) for the things that must be done from time to time to keep a school system running.

The whole problem stems from the organizational structure of a school system. School systems are organized on the line of authority model of business and industry. It may even more generally follow the line and staff organizational plan of the armed services.

Theoretically, according to these organizational models, each school administrator or supervisor is responsible for more work than he can personally do. Therefore, he delegates part of his responsibilities to others, who are then said to report to him. If this network is considered from the center (the superintendent) to the periphery of the organization (the teacher), then this outer direction would be called the Line of Delegation. In the reverse, considering the organization of a typical school system from the subordinate inward to the person who delegates responsibility, the same network is called the Line of Accountability.

Such a plan of organization is very useful. Some form of the Line of Delegation/Accountability (Figure 10-1) is used in every school district because of its characteristics, which are:

1. To designate professional positions, such as: Superintendent of Schools, Assistant Superintendents, Supervisors and Directors, Principals, Teachers.
2. To show relationships of people to authority, such as: Assistant Superintendents are subordinate to Superintendents; Supervisors and Directors are subordinate to Assistant Superintendents; Principals may be subordinate to Supervisors and Directors; Teachers are subordinate to Principals.
3. To display the chain of command (delegation), such as: delegation of authority from Superintendent to Assistant Superintendent; from Assistant Superintendent to Directors or Supervisors; from Directors or Supervisors to Principals; from Principals to Teachers.
4. To show designation of positions of accountability in line positions.

Nearly all social scientists who have studied organization recognize that the In-Line Structure is a normative fiction. It does not describe what exists, but what managers think ought to exist. Any management text demonstrates this by discussing the "formal" organization as different from the "informal" organization. Observations show that most people in an organization have work to do coming from many different sources and not just from one. In the whole realm of profession-client relationships as applicable to student-teacher relationships, the in-line organization breaks down. While official accountability is a feeling of obligation for the accomplishment of work delegated by one's "superior," most school people also feel and should feel accountable

EXAMPLES OF FLOW OF DELEGATION AND OF ACCOUNTABILITY

Delegation Flow	Accountability Flow
↓	↑
Superintendent	Superintendent
↓	↑
Assistant Superintendent	Assistant Superintendent
↓	↑
Supervisor or Director	Supervisor or Director
↓	↑
Principals	Principals
↓	↑
Teachers	Teachers

Figure 10-1

to others in the organization and to their clients (students) for whom they provide service.

The seemingly straightforward concept of the Line of Delegation or the Chain of Command turns out, in fact, to be a tremendously oversimplified picture of organizational structure. Moreover, this concept takes care of only one aspect of accountability, that of the subordinate to a person in a superior authoritative position.

This organizational chart concept of In-Line Delegation fails on several counts.

1. It does not show how the "informal" organization works.
2. It does not show the accountability of the hierarchical positions to those lower on the chart.
3. It depersonalizes the people in the organization by making them stereotyped positions in boxes on a chart.
4. It oversimplifies the complex nature of an organization.
5. It restricts communication to "going through channels," sometimes through several levels, before a decision can be obtained. For example: A teacher wants to order a special set of supplies. He must ask the principal, who in turn asks a director, who in turn asks the assistant superintendent, who in turn requests permission from the superintendent.
6. It restricts information "up the organization": Each person in the upper hierarchical position receives only that information which the people reporting to him want him to have or think he needs. They may deliberately hold back information they do not want him to have and thus protect their own position as indispensable. If a middle person does not let others

have as much information as he has, he cannot be bypassed in the decision process. This technique is common in all bureaucracies.

7. It promotes suspicion and rumor.

The following illustration is an account of how the preparation of a decision matrix helped solve these problems in one rather large school system.

The school system had for many years been organized as a single unit with all principals reporting directly to the central office. The central administrative officers had naturally collected around themselves a group of staff officers to assist in making decisions about the conduct of the district as a whole. Dissatisfaction existed because of the centralization of authority. School principals felt they were too far removed from the decision structure of the district and thus unable to make properly the decisions which affected the conduct of their schools. The teachers also felt very far from the central office and the ''we—they'' syndrome developed.

The district reorganized on an area basis by appointing administrative directors as intermediaries with responsibility for coordinating the operation of a small cluster of schools.

The new organization had been in operation almost a year before confusion became evident and factions started to form in an effort to get or maintain power in the decision process. All former procedures had been interrupted and new understandings about who was accountable for what had to be established.

The line of accountability simply did not prove sufficient guidance to those responsible for decisions along the line.

To solve this problem the superintendent wisely established a problem-solving workshop for the central office specialists, the area administrators, and representative principals and teachers. After an introduction to the problem, the superintendent presented to the group a consulting resource person to assist them in further defining their problems and organizing to solve them. The resource person was hired from a university and selected because of his competence in group processes and understanding of processes for fixing responsibility for decisions. The presence of the resource person had many advantages. He had an aura of neutrality about him and thus reduced any suspicion of self-interest. The superintendent was also freed from the responsibility of conducting the meetings, thus putting himself on an equal status with others as a learner and participant in the problem-solving workshop. When he was needed to give assurances and sanction to decisions, he was available to do so.

The resource person introduced the decision-making charting technique in its simplest form by explaining that every action needs someone to initiate it and to have the responsibility for carrying it through to completion. He let the symbol Z stand for this responsibility.

Every important action which involves other people also needs the consultation of two kinds, those who will be highly affected by the decision and those who have expert knowledge which should be considered. He let the letter *C* stand for this function.

Every action which requires accountability on the part of an administrator requires his approval. This sanctioning function of giving approval was designated by the letter *A*.

Finally, many people must be informed of the decision so that they can do what they must do as a result of the decision.

Thus, the key symbols in charting decisions are:

(*Z*) Needs to start and carry out the task.
(*C*) Must be consulted for advice.
(*A*) Must approve the action.
(*I*) Must be informed of the decision.

Notice the restrictive words attached to each symbol. If the process is to work, then it *must* be followed. When agreement is reached as to who should properly participate in the process, then this person *must* be either consulted, give his approval, or be informed, whichever the case may be.

With these symbols in mind, the mechanics of preparing a decision chart become simple. The group process for preparing the chart, however, is not simple. A chart is of no use if people won't follow it. Therefore, the process of preparing the chart must involve those most concerned with the decision.

In the case at hand, feelings were taut. It was a case of central office supervisory personnel pitted against area administrators, each of whom was either trying to retain or gain power in the decision-making process. The resource person decided to give the group some practice in charting decision-making responsibility. The example taken was the replacement of an electric range for a home economics class. This may not seem the most momentous type of decision in the world. It is tremendously important, however, to people within an organization.

Who has authority to spend money is always symbolic of power. If a principal has this authority, it is proof of his autonomy. If the new intermediate administrators can give final approval, their positions have then been recognized as essential. On the other hand, the old system had put the authority in the hands of central office personnel, experts in their field. If they lost this final symbol of authority, they felt their positions were threatened.

Also, the purchase of equipment is extremely important instructionally. The equipment is the concrete evidence of all the planning that goes into the instructional program.

Finally, equipment is visible to all. Businessmen who visit the school see it and may question the economics of purchasing policies. Often Boards of

Education and superintendents are judged by the procedures they use in purchasing such mundane things as ranges for home economics classes.

Who must be involved then in the decision to replace an electric range? Certainly the home economics teacher, who knows of the need and is to use it. The principal of the school knows of comparative needs of his school. (Is a stove more important for the home economics room than a piano for the music room?) The central office home economics supervisor, who knows of the educational requirements for good equipment, should influence the decision. The area director, who must coordinate all of the expenditures of the area and prepare budgets, must in some way reflect comparative needs. The superintendent, who has to authorize all expenditures for major equipment, would need to authorize the purchase. Finally, the purchasing agent, who must secure competitive prices and issue the purchase order, must be informed of the need.

All of these functions were put on one axis of the following chart in Figure 10-2, while those concerned were put on another axis. The symbols are those which were supplied in the first attempt by the group. They assumed that the Z might stand for the most power and therefore gave that power to the superintendent. They also assumed that everyone along the line should have something to say about the process.

For the practice exercise in preparing a chart, the resource person divided the workshop participants into small groups of seven or eight to put the symbols into the blank matrix. Each group contained a cross section of people from supervisory personnel to teachers. After putting their chart together, each group reported their recommendations to the group as a whole.

As the reports were made and displayed on large charts around the room, several patterns became evident (See Figure 10-2). Nearly every group put most of the Z's with the superintendent. After all, he was the person whom they perceived to have the authority to start and carry out action, and the role was perceived as a high administrative function. Also, nearly every person in an administrative office was given an A for approval or a C for consultation. This was a misconception of the initiation, approval and consultation roles.

To put the Z with the superintendent meant that he had to carry out all of the tasks and most action would require his initiation. Also, to give the A (approval) down the line would require the superintendent's actions to be approved by principals, area administrators and supervisors, an unlikely situation. It became evident that the Z and A roles should be reversed. Someone down the line should initiate and carry through most actions, while the superintendent should give the necessary approval.

Also, the number of consultations and approvals along the line became unreasonable. As one administrator said, "If I had to get this many approvals and hold this many consultations, I could never get a new stove for the home economics room." He was right!

A MISCONCEPTION OF ROLES
IN DECISION MAKING

	teacher	principal	area director	supervisor	supt.	purchasing agent
1. Designation of need	A	A	A	C	Z	I
2. Checking comparative needs for the school	C	A	A	A	Z	
3. Checking of comparative needs for the area	C	C	Z	C	A	
4. Checking of educational specifications	C	A	A	C	Z	
5. Recommending purchase	A	A	A	A	Z	
6. Issuing purchase order				C	Z	I
7. Verifying receipt of merchandise and authorizing payment	I	C	A	A	Z	C

Figure 10-2

The resource person for the workshop wisely introduced to the group the notions of negotiation, delegation and trust. The group decided that no single action should require more than two C's (consultations) or more than two A's (approvals). Others would simply have to be satisfied with being informed of the action and trust the procedure as reasonable and fair. The decision of who would do this in each case became one for negotiation, with some give and take and much trust.

This was an important decision for the group. It could only be reached by group interaction. It also removed the individuals from primary concern with their own roles and put them in the objective position of looking at "process." This procedure also influenced attitudes of the group by giving them new perspectives of process vs. individual concerns.

The groups then went back into sessions and redrew their decision matrices, following obviously needed restrictions. In a spirit of trust and negotiation, the chart was greatly simplified with all roles having some influence, but with less concern for each person being able to approve every action of every other person.

The model chart was also generalized to encompass the replacement of all major equipment of the district since the procedure would be essentially the same for purchasing a range or for a new movie projector. Some new people, such as teachers' advisory committees, were introduced to make the procedure complete.

The chart, as negotiated, is shown in Fig. 10-3.

REPLACEMENT OF MAJOR EQUIPMENT DECISION MATRIX[3]

Decision Points	Classroom Teacher	Principal	Area Administrator	Supervisor	Teacher Advisory Committee	Superintendent	Purchasing Clerk
1. Designation of need	Z	A	I	I			
2. Checking comparative needs for the school	I	Z	A	C			
3. Checking comparative needs of the area	I	I	Z	C		I	
4. Preparation of budget		C	Z	I		A	
5. Preparing educational specifications				Z	C	Z	
6. Recommending purchase	I	I	Z	C		A	
7. Issuing purchase order		I	I	C		A	Z
8. Verifying receipt and authorizing payment		Z				A	I

Figure 10-3

1. You will note in Fig. 10-3 that the teacher designated a need but the approval rested with the principal, who informs the area administrator and the supervisor that the new equipment was requested.
2. The principal conducts a comparative needs survey of his building and prioritizes the need. In doing this he consults the supervisor regarding the adequacy of the present equipment in comparison with general district standards.

---

[3]John L. Wallen, *Charting the Decision Making Structure of an Organization*, Program Report: Improving Teaching Competencies Program. Northwest Regional Educational Laboratory, Portland, Oregon, 1971, p. 2.

3. The area administrator conducts a comparative needs survey of his area, and prioritizes the needs after again consulting with appropriate supervisors as to the adequacy of existing equipment. He informs the teacher, the principal and the superintendent of the needs lists.
4. The area budget is prepared by the area administrator after consultation with the principals. He informs the supervisor and requests approval of the budget from the superintendent.
5. The supervisor is given the responsibility for preparing the educational specifications for the equipment. This is done in consultation with an advisory committee of teachers. The superintendent must approve the specifications.
6. The actual requisition is made by the area administrator for purchase of all major equipment. He consults the supervisor and informs the teachers and principal.
7. The purchase order is written by the purchasing clerk after consultation with the supervisor and obtaining approval of the superintendent. Others are informed of the action.
8. When the merchandise is delivered, the principal acknowledges it and informs the purchasing clerk, who in turn gets the approval of the superintendent to pay for it.

This process resolved most of the feelings of conflict within the group used for illustration, and factions began to disappear as new insight was gained of the appropriate and legitimate roles of others. The above chart was accepted by the whole group. It was recorded and became a model for other important decisions which would follow. Many an administrator thereafter was heard to suggest, "Let's prepare a decision matrix for this new situation so that we all will understand how the decision will be made."

The technique of charting decisions has several advantages:

1. It resolves conflict in the exercise of authority by making clear the degree of influence that is required for each position.
2. It builds confidence in and respect for the legitimate roles to be played by each individual along the line of accountability.
3. It teaches the group to negotiate the degree of influence each should rightfully exercise in the decision process. If the system is to work, some authority must be passed along to others.
4. It builds trust in due process. Since those who are concerned most with the decision participate in the decision, each person, through his interaction, becomes better acquainted with his colleagues and gains respect for their area of competence and rightful degree of accountability.
5. It clearly fixes accountability for action to be taken or followed. No one can claim ignorance or misunderstanding of his role.

6. It provides a set of procedures which can be built into an administrative handbook for future use.
7. The process of consultation becomes clarified. Consultants such as supervisors rarely have authority. Their authority rests in the expertness in their field. Their accountability is to those they must serve by giving expert advice.

GUIDELINES FOR PREPARING A DECISION MATRIX

1. The preparation of a decision matrix should be a group process, at least in the initial stages. This gives each person an opportunity to influence the way decisions are made.
2. All required activities should be listed so that a clear set of functions can be designated. For example, in purchasing major equipment, the function of preparing educational specifications could easily be overlooked, unless it is provided for as a required function. Of course, when such specifications are once approved, they can be used until a need for a new set becomes evident.
3. When the functions are agreed upon, the persons who should participate or be informed should be designated across the top of the chart. This should include all persons who have either a legitimate concern for what is done or who have a special competence which can be utilized in the process.
4. The designation of kind of influence is by symbol.
   Z Needs to start and carry out the task.
   C Must be consulted for advice.
   A Must approve the action.
   I Must be informed of the decision.
5. Once agreed upon, the procedure *must* be followed; that is, a person listed for consultation C must not only be consulted, but must also give or obtain advice. Generally, there should be no more than two C's for a function.
6. Generally, only one person should initiate an activity and have the responsibility for carrying this out. This Z position is usually the one closest to the problem.
7. The A position for authorization is both the most powerful position and designates the person finally accountable. This person, in turn, holds others in the process accountable for their designated functions. There should generally be no more than two A's for any one function.
8. The designation of I is for all of those who need to know. Usually all positions will be informed when the sequence is completed.

No matrix can solve all problems of conflicting administrative authority, but a matrix can go a long way in the clarification of roles and responsibilities.

Any routine function in a school district can be charted. The process can be used at the local school level, the area level or the school district level; it can be used at any level where a set of decisions are made.

The decision charting technique is not a replacement for the organizational structure of a district. The usual organizational chart showing hierarchical relationships is still necessary. The decision matrix can, however, supplement this organizational structure with an underpinning of agreed-upon processes which make the organization work.

SUMMARY

There are formal and informal characteristics of all organizations. The formal characteristics are the hierarchical arrangements for delegating authority. The informal characteristics are those which explain how things get done.

Members of organizations who do not understand how things get done are prey to rumor and discontent. They often explain the actions of others in terms of their motives. Also, accountability is not possible when there is not a clear picture of who does what and how they participate in decisions.

This chapter presents a technique for displaying just who participates in specific decisions within the organization. Figure 10-4 illustrates how a decision matrix can be used in a specific sequence of activities necessary to the replacement of major equipment within a school district. A set of symbols explains just who (by position—not name) does what. A Z designates who must initiate and carry through the action. A C designates who must be consulted before the action is taken. A designates who must approve the action, and I designates who must be informed.

The technique has many advantages:

1. It resolves conflicts about who is responsible for what.
2. It builds respect for legitimate roles for each position.
3. It teaches the group to negotiate its roles within a decision process.
4. It builds trust in due process.
5. It fixes accountability at the task level.
6. It helps to build a set of procedures.
7. The consulting role becomes clarified.

11

Building Competence in Others for Management Development

Most people in an organization want to do a good job. Some psychologists even go so far as to say that most people do as well as they can given the limitations of their perception of need, the knowledge they have, and their skill or effectiveness in getting things done. The school principal who is arbitrary and dictatorial behaves that way because he perceives his role as that of a decision maker and a director of other peoples' actions. The supervisor who individually selects a new course of study and calls a meeting to explain it to teachers may have a great deal of knowledge about what constitutes a good course of study but may lack the knowledge of the whole process of influencing others.

A school system must provide means for staff growth and development, which takes into account the cross section of needs of its total staff, particularly its leadership staff. The point here is that those in leadership positions are so influential within the organization that they can almost assure or conversely prevent good activities and growth of others.

This chapter deals with the elements of a good professional growth program for the school leadership group. Through the discussions and illustrations presented, you should become familiar with the new knowledge which has been generated about how people grow and develop, the techniques for effecting change in others, and the characteristics of an organization which promotes continuous growth and development of its members.

As an illustration of how these elements interact in a school system, let's look at a new superintendent of a moderate sized district who was selected to effect change in the district. The school Board had screened applicants very carefully to select a leader who would introduce modern, up-to-date instructional techniques in its suburban district. The Board represented the professional elements of the community, and they valued good education for their children. Yet they had observed a growing dropout rate and arbitrary enforcement of administrative rules and regulations without regard to the effect on individuals. The main job of the new superintendent was to guide the school system toward an instructional system which would be more responsive to the current concerns of young people and which would involve them in a meaningful way in their own educational process. In other words, the school Board wanted a school system which had vitality, was open to new educational approaches, and which assured children of the opportunity to achieve their maximum educational potential.

The district, being of middle to upper socioeconomic status, had provided well for its schools. The buildings were modern and the staff was well paid, yet the achievement was mediocre and the students reacted indifferently or rebelliously to their schools. Also, the teachers were dissatisfied and let their dissatisfactions be known within the district.

As pointed out before, the district had been generous in its opportunities for staff. There was a leave of absence provided for senior teachers and administrators providing monetary incentive for college courses taken and rewarded for those who obtained higher academic degrees. Each principal, supervisor and department chairman was permitted to attend, at district expense, one annual meeting of the professional organization of his choice. On the face of it, the professional growth program was good, yet something was wrong.

The superintendent made his own observations. He observed principals in faculty meetings and teaching in the classroom, looked into past opportunities for professional growth within the district, and discussed administrative techniques with supervisors.

The superintendent first observed a principal lecturing a staff on flexible scheduling and trying to influence them to go along with a new plan which he had learned about at a national meeting. The faculty was less than impressed. They wanted their autonomy in the classroom and were unwilling to do the hard work of planning the details of the program. They were generally threatened by the whole idea.

The superintendent then observed a teacher in the classroom who had been to a National Science Foundation workshop on the "new" biology. The teacher, after two months, was giving up the new approaches in frustration for several reasons. His colleagues couldn't understand why he was abandoning the traditional approaches to teaching biology. His department chairman was concerned that the students might not pass the traditional college board examination in science. His principal could not understand why he needed all of the new equipment for which there had been no budget. The students were "turned on'' by the new course and were enthusiastic about their level of participation and self-determination afforded them. Yet the teacher was about to abandon his efforts. There were simply too many obstacles to overcome.

The superintendent talked to a central office administrator in his office. This administrator had the reputation of being arbitrary and insensitive. A parent's call came to the administrator about a violation of the dress code in one of the schools. The administrator took the call, was sympathetic to the parent and assured the parent on the spot that something would be done about it. He then called the school and directed the principal to enforce the dress code. When the observing superintendent asked the administrator about his actions, the administrator assured him that he had a reputation to maintain. His reputation, as he perceived it, was that he was one who could make decisions, was always prompt in solving problems, and was fair and impartial. His overall concept of himself was that he was sensitive to the needs of òthers and very kind and supportive of his subordinates. The principal, on the other hand, perceived him as arbitrary, abrupt and nonsupportive.

The superintendent then observed a new elementary principal recently selected as one who wanted to share decision-making processes and to meaningfully involve his staff in all pertinent decisions. The teachers had a different expectation of what a principal should be. The principal wanted to be a participant-leader. The teachers had a stereotype role perception of a principal who should be a decision maker and the director of the school. They thus resisted efforts on the part of the principal to involve them in decisions which they thought should be his. They thought of him as a ''weak'' principal who wouldn't assume his proper functions. Yet the teachers liked him as a person. They thought of him as smart, kind and considerate, but did not think he was a good principal.

The superintendent's final observation was of a lecturer presenting an inservice class to a group of teachers. He was talking about processes of curriculum construction. Teachers had enrolled in the class so that they could get a credit in curriculum and thus advance on the salary schedule. The lecturer, a professor at a local college, tried to get participation on the part of teachers in preparing a prototype curriculum for a new course. The teachers were not enthusiastic about the course. They would prefer that the professors simply lecture on good curriculum processes and give them a test at the end of the course. They were not willing to work on a prototype which they thought would have little value to them personally in their work.

The superintendent was able to pinpoint these observations and derive several conclusions which he wanted to consider when he planned his staff development program.

1. The participation of staff members in college classes and national

meetings brought them a great deal of knowledge about good educational procedures. Most of the leaders wanted to improve their schools, but as the superintendent put it, "they were all thumbs" when they went about trying to effect change. They did not possess the skills to achieve what they set out to achieve.

2. Sending a single teacher to a seminar or year-long institute to bring back a new program and put it into effect was not a successful approach to change. The teacher returning to the school setting becomes a "lonely" person who cannot achieve his goals because of lack of mutual support from his colleagues and because of lack of facilitation of his efforts by his supervisors. He gradually becomes a marginal member of the group. At first they question him and try to understand his program. Finally, communication is cut off and he becomes isolated in the group without support from his colleagues.

3. A person is a poor judge of the effect of his own behavior on others. Often a person has an entirely different perception of the effect of his behavior on others than do those who are affected by his behavior.

4. People have stereotyped perceptions of the proper roles for each position in an organization. People can like a person very much, yet become impatient if he does not play his professional role as they think it should be played. For example, when we go to a service station to get something done to our car, we expect the attendant simply to do what his role demands. We really don't care to know whether he left home without breakfast because his wife was ill, just as long as he services our car and we can get on with our business. If a person deviates too much from his role, he is not perceived to be good in that role. He can only change his role if he takes others along with him and if they also modify their expectations.

5. Teachers want to work in real problems of concern to them. They are wary of any effort to involve them in "fun and games" which do not have a direct application to a real need as they perceive it.

As we analyze each of the above conclusions, we come to the realization that each is a condition of human perception and interaction.

In planning an effective professional growth program, the superintendent must call upon the developments of the new social science processes in social psychology. Many new discoveries have been made by social psychologists about how to teach people effectively in their human interaction. Traditionally those who have studied human interaction have set up experiments with small groups, usually with an experimental and a control group. One variable, and only one, was then introduced to the experimental group and withheld from the control group. If the experimental group responded at a significantly higher level than the control group, then the variable was said to be an important element in human interaction. During the late 1940's and the 1950's a great collection of data was gathered about how individuals function in a group situation. Such experimentation verified by replication emerged as a whole new approach to training in the field of interaction processes.

Yet the first courses provided in colleges to teach people to be better human interactors were not successful. The courses, presented in lecture/reading/demonstration form, prepared people with much information about human interaction, but with little skill in actually doing it. Learning about interaction was simply not like learning how to do it effectively.

The first concentrated efforts to overcome the deficiencies of the "telling how-to" method was the development of "laboratory training" in the 50's and 60's. This is based upon group interaction techniques wherein participants actually go through the necessary processes. The whole question of how you learn effective group behavior or group leadership skills was the focus of the effort. It was known that a person simply cannot learn these new techniques by drill or rote. It was also known that individuals cannot simply find it out for themselves, because they do not get sufficient feedback about how they affect others.

It was discovered that we must have some kind of an educational context and experience in which we can be helped to discover the constructive aspects of our own behavior in relation to other people. This is essentially what is meant by the laboratory method of interpersonal relations or human relations training, or just simply process training. The key essence of laboratory training (learning) is that participants examine the behavior that occurs in the learning situation together and try to find out what it means, and that any particular thing that happens, any interaction, is the basis of learning.

The early efforts at these endeavors were held in Bethel, Maine, and are now generally available everywhere. Various names have been given to these training programs. These include group process training, encounter groups, and T (training) groups or sensitivity training—all associated with an organization known as the National Training Laboratories (NTL) or with individual freelance trainers.

From these early efforts there have emerged many variations of group training processes. Some have been highly effective and some such efforts have generated a great deal of criticism because of unorthodox methods.

There has been a great evolution in the whole process of group training. From the early beginning of open encounter, there have been developed highly sophisticated training systems (packages) for specific purposes. These training systems have been developed in national educational laboratories such as the Northwest Regional Educational Laboratory in Portland, Oregon, and the Far West Laboratory in San Francisco. Systems have also been developed by individual educational psychologists and by private groups, such as the Human Development Institute, Atlanta, Georgia. These new systems differ greatly from the open encounter methods in several respects.

A learning system differs from other group training approaches in that the goals of the training provided are to assure certain specific understandings and skills on the part of trainees. In other words, the trainee will develop certain predetermined competencies that he didn't have before, but these will be competencies in the utilization of certain processes for application in many situations rather than solutions to problems per se. For example, one system of training might be designed to assure competencies in communication skills on the part of the participants. These would include such skills as how to ask a question so that it elicits exactly the kind of information the questioner is seeking, or the technique of paraphrasing to assure mutual understanding. The group is used as a laboratory for practice. Learning systems are always positive and helpful. Participants never experience the "encounter" or "confrontation," which is often the result of the unstructured open groups that one hears so much about these days.

Well designed instructional systems, such as those developed by laboratories, provide a leader's manual and participant "handouts" with explanations, simulations and problem statements. These materials have been carefully tested so that in a given time and sequence the objectives, as stated, can be attained by the participants, if the system is used as designed.

The encounter groups, on the other hand, are open and depend on a highly skilled leader to give guidance to the group, while the new instructional system packages can be successfully led by a person of intermediate skills who has successfully completed the training himself.

The encounter approaches are not task-oriented, while the new instructional systems are planned to teach a specific set of skills, such as interpersonal communication, problem solving, or systematic planning.

Actually, the only similarity between the new instructional systems and the sensitivity training is that each requires some form of interaction with others and some system of feedback, so that the participants always know how well they are doing and can continuously test their skills.

Another difference is that sensitivity training often relies on high emotional impact situations and negative interaction as a basis for its training. The new instructional systems more often are designed to give only positive and reinforcing feedback to the learner.

ORGANIZATIONAL DEVELOPMENT AND MANAGEMENT

A second body of knowledge being worked on by social psychologists is needed by the superintendent. It is that generated around the topic of organizational development and management, such as developed at the University of Michigan Institute of Human Development. Both organizational development and management imply staff growth. If you are going to have an effective, developing organization, it stands to reason that you must help the people in it develop in order to function well in it.

Management science requires that organizational change start at the top. It does little good to try to bring a change down the line if the organization itself does not support it. We saw this in the case of the teacher who tried to introduce a new biological science course. Top management must facilitate and accommodate change or it cannot be long lasting.

After starting at the top, the organizational development effort must be systemic, that is, it must affect the entire system (its people, its structure, and its environment).

The approach must above all be based on data. What do we know about the organization, what are our goals, and what must we do to achieve them?

Finally, the approach must lead to personal satisfaction. Will people feel good about themselves and their relationships to others as a result of the organizational change?

The classical Western Electric "Hawthorne" experiment illustrated how production increased because workers participated in decisions. As the lighting was changed, production increased. In this experiment, each new innovation in which the workers participated improved production. This kind of personal satisfaction is essential in any organizational change. Otherwise, the desired effect cannot be maintained.

With these two major developments in mind, the superintendent in this case study began with his top administrative groups to involve them in the planning of the kind of organization they wanted to be a part of. He arranged for the principals and supervisory personnel to go on a weekend retreat in order to remove them from their daily cares and help put them in a relaxed, responsive mood.

The futures game: As a beginning exercise the group was divided into clusters of four or five to play the futures game.

Each group was asked to respond successively to three questions.

1. Consider the next 10 to 20 years. What will be the conditions in the world at that time which will affect our school system?
2. What skills and attributes will be needed to exist and live effectively in such a world?
3. What are the requirements of an educational system which can provide these skills and attributes for this emerging world?

This simple exercise helped the administrators move toward a new perspective, one removed from immediate problems toward a more global concept.

The conditions identified by the groups covered many areas: personal, social, economic and political considerations. These had to do with the whole area of personal freedom and choice; the emergence of social systems to include minority groups in an effective way; changes in family structure; rapid expansion of technology; economic changes; the move toward more government control; more frequent changes in occupations in the life of an individual; increase in leisure time and reduction of the work week.

It was generally agreed among the groups of administrators that these conditions would give many more choices to the individual, and that more judgment and self-direction would be required of him. Therefore, the skills and attributes which will be needed by the present school children and youth should include: (1) the ability to deal with information, (2) the ability to make decisions and (3) the self-understandings necessary to give them the assurances they will need to stand as individuals. Above all, students should become lifelong active learners, continually re-evaluating themselves and redirecting their energies as they move through life and progress through the various evolutionary stages of becoming ever more perceptive and competent individuals.

With these things in mind the group then looked at question number three. What are the requirements of an educational system which can provide these skills and attributes for this world? The administrators listed many, all of which centered on more active participation in the educative process by learners.

As the participants discussed the role of the school, they agreed on the following as worthy characteristics of a good school system.

1. Assure that students achieve minimal knowledge, skills and attitudinal competence necessary to become participating members of society.
2. Maximize the opportunities for students to develop as individuals.
3. Help students become active in their own learning processes.
4. Make learning a personal matter for each student.
5. Help teachers make better use of the tools of learning.
6. Help teachers plan for educational improvement.
7. Use the community as a learning environment.
8. Review the educational objectives to be sure that they included some of the learning processes as well as subject matter.
9. Help teachers gain more skill in using good teaching-learning processes in the classroom.

The principals and supervisors next turned their attention to the question of how they could achieve these results. They listed such questions as:

1. Does our present organization accommodate this kind of a school system?
2. What leadership skills do I need in my role to achieve these goals?

3. How do I get my teachers involved so that they too will value and work toward these goals?
4. How fast can we move? What are reasonable expectations?

It was decided that teachers too need the experience of a retreat—that they should be involved in these decisions. It was also decided that the district should divert some of its staff development money to process training, not just content classes.

The superintendent, through this futures game exercise, had achieved a significant educational growth on the part of his leadership group. He had done this in a setting which was conducive to promoting new perceptions. Some aside observations should be noted. As the retreat progressed participants became more free and easy in their interpersonal exchanges. More references were made to each other as "Mary" or "George" as people felt more comfortable with each other. Members felt that they were members of a team, each contributing to a significant effort. They started to view the role of the superintendent as a leadership and facilitation role instead of a controlling authority figure. They respected him for this new role.

This case study illustrates how problems of change within an organization can be analyzed and a program begun to establish a new direction in developing staff competence and organizational change. Any school system which makes the kinds of beginnings described here should be carried along by the new momentum, excitement and insights gained.

No superintendent or principal can carry forward the whole professional growth program by himself. He needs to gain some of these skills himself, and sometimes he should be the leader of the group, but sometimes he should be a participant. He will also need the resources of skilled trainers and training systems to bring more depth into the problem-solving processes. Also, the whole job cannot be done at once. An organization is a dynamic thing, constantly changing and adapting itself to new situations and needs. As people change within the organization, new insights and problems are brought into it. The key here is to keep the organization moving in good directions rather than undesirable ones. Also, change is not an orderly process. An organization will move ahead on broad fronts, making significant thrusts in new directions from time to time. The movements should be coordinated as much as possible so that the total organization can always accommodate and support worthy movements.

The resources for a good leadership management improvement system are many and varied. Not all persons within an organization will need or respond to the same treatment. Therefore, the professional growth program should be diversified and should allow for individual variations.

In the case at point, the superintendent maintained the good features of the professional growth program already available. The provisions for college training, district inservice classes and attendance at conferences were all good.

Some of the members of the leadership group definitely wanted to participate in open sensitivity-type training sessions. Some, on the other hand, felt threatened by such encounters. Most of the group felt they would profit from training in communication skills of the type developed as a tested instructional system.

Both at the district-wide level and at the school level, some training in systematic approaches was included. These programs assisted participants in learning the techniques of needs assessment, goal setting, problem identification, research utilization and problem solution. A strong emphasis was also placed on programs to help individuals understand the nature of orgnaizations and processes of organizational change.

Finally, teachers began to have a wider variety of opportunities to improve their day-to-day teaching competencies through taking training in some of the new classroom interaction techniques, which made them more aware and more skillful in their daily interaction with students.

Many colleges and universities are incorporating these new training systems into their curriculums, especially at the graduate level for those who are specializing in leadership roles. Most often, however, such training must be secured by groups in the field, and many are only effective if conducted in a school or district setting where the group that works together learns together, and local problems are dealt with. Therefore, school systems such as the one we have been discussing must make up their own training programs from the many pieces available to them.

SUMMARY

This chapter pointed out the broader dimensions of the problems of staff development within an organizational structure.

It pointed out the deficiencies in usual staff development programs which center only on individuals within the organization, and which deliver mainly the traditional information giving instructional procedures. The reader should have become aware of the importance of staff development programs which are responsive to organizational needs as well as the individual needs.

Two major developments in staff development potentials have resulted from the social psychological studies of human interaction in group situations and from the dimensions of organizational change and management. The first group of studies resulted in new and effective training techniques for individuals in group situations. These techniques range from an open encounter sensitivity training to specific instructional systems designed and tested to deliver a particular set of insights and skills to the participants.

The second set of training programs is designed to help leaders within an organization set goals, father data, and plan effective ways to improve the organization. Since organizational change and improvement results only from people in the organization working more effectively as a team, the programs are always designed to help people improve their role fulfillment.

These particular programs (organizational and management training) are less well developed at this time and are more reliant on the expertise of the trainer than are the group process instructional systems. Nevertheless, the two approaches should be used together to achieve effective change in a school system.

This chapter has not listed specific sources of training programs except to designate the types of institutions which are developing them. The specific choice must be the school system itself.

Most resource persons trained recently in social psychological techniques can put school leaders in touch with these training resources. Also, the professional literature is including more and more references to these programs as they are tested and made available for general use.

12

Using New Management Diagnostic Techniques for Overall School Improvement

At one time the prevailing practice in supervision was inspection. Those in a supervisory position came into a school and made judgments about its effectiveness and efficiency. Each person in a supervisory position had his own criteria for judgment. Sometimes these criteria were shared with those being inspected and sometimes not.

This approach to supervision was based upon the assumption that the supervisor had superior knowledge and was able to evaluate the needs of a school or teacher and direct the solution.

When this approach was applied to the classroom, it was sometimes known as the "mother hen" approach. The supervisor attempted to "make over" the teacher in his own image and create another teacher "just like me."

What was needed were effective techniques, applicable to a total school situation, to assure that judgments were made upon adequate data, and that those being supervised could share in the decisions as to what course of action they would follow in improving their effectiveness and also be permitted to achieve the desired goals according to their best individual styles.

Often the problems faced in schools are not so much the problems of individuals, but the problems of how the organization functions as a whole, and how the individuals within it relate to others.

This chapter will present and discuss the emerging techniques which are giving those in supervisory positions more adequate and objective data for use with their clients in the improvement of their roles within the total organization. These are the new institutional diagnostic techniques which help to provide accurate information about the problems faced in a school or a total school district, and they provide a key to the action necessary to help solve knotty problems in a total school organization.

These techniques will be presented and discussed by the use of a case study of Tom Bennett, principal, whose performance is being reviewed by the director of elementary education in a moderate-sized school district. The situation is as follows:

Tom Bennett had been with the district 12 years before becoming a principal three years ago. He was a highly creative and original teacher. The first year as principal he was very active with his teachers. He established several curriculum committees and assisted two teachers in carrying out some very creative teaching units about which he received much publicity. Two traditional teachers complained to the superintendent about being overworked by the principal. The two teachers who did the work for which he received publicity were bitter about it and complained to their colleagues.

Tom began having fewer teachers meetings and started spending most of his time in his office tending to routine activities.

Generally, the atmosphere in the school was becoming tense and communication among the staff had decreased.

Tom had said to the elementary director that perhaps he wasn't cut out to be a principal.

The community was also beginning to recognize that the school did not have a good atmosphere for learning. It was evident that the staff was not working effectively together and were openly critical of each other and of the principal.

There are several techniques which a supervising director can employ to help Tom with his problems. The first is an agreed upon set of goals of what Tom should achieve in a given amount of time and how he should go about achieving them.

Next, a plan of action should be agreed upon. This plan of action must include:

1. Statements of milestones to be achieved.
2. The criteria upon which achievement of milestones toward the goals will be judged.
3. The enumeration of resources to be provided.
4. Clarification of the support or facilitating role to be played by the supervising director.

The general goals agreed upon were:

Goal 1. Tom and the director agree that a good beginning would be for him to find out more about the expectations of his staff, in terms of his role in decision making and their expectations of their own roles.

Goal 2. The two also agree that from this diagnosis several problems should be identified for analysis.

Goal 3. After the identification of the problems, one or more problems should be selected for concentrated efforts on the part of the principal.

Goal 4. The two will then agree upon some indicators (measurable or observable things) that will tell both of them the degree of success attained.

Goal 5. They will work together on a plan of action for the achievement of these goals.

Tom, of course, did not have knowledge and competence in all of these areas of diagnosis and prescription. His training in organizational problem solving was limited to a few courses in school administration. Also, it was recognized that Tom had already contributed to the strained relationship with his teachers and that he needed someone to intervene occasionally from the outside. On the other hand, whatever action was taken should clearly build Tom's leadership image and capacity as a principal. Therefore, he had to carry the bulk of the leadership in this effort himself.

A PLAN OF ACTION

The director and Tom therefore agreed upon a plan of action, with each spelling out his responsibilities.
Tom would:

1. Study some publications on organizational climate and management.[1]
2. Examine techniques for the diagnosis of school climate.
3. Meet with his supervising director at agreed upon times to review his plans and approaches.
4. Move ahead on the whole problem of improving the professional climate of his school.

Tom's supervisor will:

1. Help Tom locate the best publications on organizational climate and

---

[1]Example of such a publication: Robert S. Fox, Richard Schmuck, Elmer Van Egmond, Miriam Ritro, Charles Jung, *Diagnosing Professional Climate of Schools*, NTL Learning Resources Corp., Inc., Fairfax, Virginia 22030.

management available like the one cited before in Item 1.

2. Help Tom secure the instruments, like those to follow in this chapter, and learn the techniques he needs to diagnose the school climate.
3. Provide funds from the budget to get Tom some outside consultation and materials.
4. Promptly review Tom's plans, give sanction where necessary and suggestions where needed.
5. Will *not*, however, make Tom's decisions for him nor intervene in his relationships with his staff unless invited to do so, or unless a crisis develops.

It should be noted here that both the elementary director and Tom knew the steps to be taken by each. It should also be noted that Tom was free to pursue the goals according to his best judgment, but with the assistance of his director. Tom was held fully accountable for his activities, and their success or failure rested upon him. It was recognized, however, that he could not achieve these goals without support. In this case, the support includes (1) advice, (2) resources, (3) sanction or approval where necessary and (4) outside consultation.

At the end of the agreed upon time limits, the director would review the progress. In the case of Tom, these reviews were to be rather frequent, but at fixed points and with specific milestones (achievement review points). Milestone review dates were established so that Tom could gear his work to specific points in the achievement of the goals. Also the criteria for judging whether or not the milestone was satisfactorily reached were made explicit.

Figure 12-1 charts the dates for the milestone review. The criteria for judging milestone achievements followed the calendar.

MILESTONES AND REVIEW

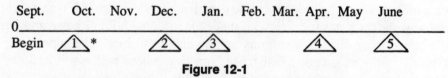

Figure 12-1

△1 Identification Milestone, October 10. When this first milestone was reached, Tom would have reviewed the literature on institutional diagnostic techniques. He would select those he wants to use.

Criteria for judgment

1. Techniques would be listed by Tom.
2. Techniques would be selected by Tom for use.

△2 Milestone, December 1. Data would have been gathered by using the techniques, and would be ready for analysis.

*Standard symbol for milestone review point

Criteria for judgment

1. The selected techniques would have been applied.
2. The data would be summarized.
3. Inferences would be drawn.

△3 Problem Selection Milestone, January 15. Using the data collected, problems would be identified with the assistance of an outside consultant.

Criteria for judgment

1. The problems would be supported by data.
2. The problems would be prioritized.
3. The selected problems to be worked upon would be indicated.

△4 Progress Milestone, April 1. A progress report toward problem solution would have been prepared by Tom for the review of the directors.

Criteria for judgment

1. Progress would be indicated on the solution of each identified problem.
2. Next steps would be indicated.

△5 Summary Milestone, June 1, A summary of the progress made would be prepared by Tom.

Criteria for judgment

1. The original goals would be reviewed.
2. Progress would be reviewed.
3. Next steps would be indicated.

This review procedure and time line were demanding but realistic because of the pressing circumstances surrounding the situation. It was progressive and explicit. It gave Tom a clear picture of his director's expectations and the criteria on which he would be judged. It also established milestones to be reached along the way and the dates for review. It made his responsibilities known and it made the supervising director's responsibilities known to him. The supervising director's role was support, assistance, sanction where necessary, and review. The criteria on which progress would be judged were indicated.

Following are three techniques for diagnosing the health of Tom's school. These techniques were prepared by the author as examples only. They are based upon models found in the literature on institutional management and diagnosis of school climates. These techniques are designed to obtain information about the way people think things are or should be. There are no norms for rating a school as good or bad on a total score basis. Institutions are healthy if the people in them think things are as they should be. Institutions are unhealthy if there is a high degree of discrepancy between how people perceive things and how they think things should be. The areas with the greatest discrepancy are those needing the most attention.

The data gathering instruments in almost every case must be tailored to the specific institution. Seldom is one applicable in its original form. The instruments presented here may be used in a school if they fit precisely. They should be modified if they don't fit. Few, if any, standards instruments of this kind are available on the market.

PERCEPTIONS OF MANAGEMENT PRACTICE
(INSTRUMENT I)

This technique is designed to find out what teachers expect of their principal as a manager and the discrepancy between their expectations and the actual situation as they perceive it to be.

> Directions to staff members: Please look at each of the management functions a principal carries on. Mark an "X" at the place on the scale indicating how desirable you believe it is for a principal to behave in this way. Then go back and mark an "O" on the scale indicating how you believe things actually are in your school.

> Assurance of anonymity: These forms may be sealed in an envelope without signatures and mailed to the statistical clerk. The response of individual staff members will not be identified. Summaries will be used by the staff later for discussion.

This instrument shows the summary responses as hypothesized for Tom. If this was truly the response of the teachers in Tom's school, it would indicate a rather bad situation. See Figure 12-2.

He was perceived as not consulting his staff before making decisions; as not delegating responsibility as often as needed; as having favorites. The areas of praise and reprimand were not considered very important, and the staff perceived him as using each about right. He obviously entertains and is a "good fellow" off the job, but the staff believes it is unimportant.

The use of Instrument I will provide data on which to base decisions. It is not a decision instrument in and of itself.

INFLUENCE

All members of an organization want to feel that they can influence it. Yet many organizational members feel trapped and helpless when it comes to influencing the decisions that are made in their organization. As pointed out in

MANAGEMENT FUNCTIONS

	Not desirable	Highly desirable	

	0 20 40 60 80 100	Discrepancy score
Consultation: Consults staff before making important decisions	0- - - - - - - - - -X	60
Praises: Praises good work	0- - - -X	20
Social: Entertains off the job	X- - - -- - --0	40
Delegation: Delegates responsibility	0- - - - - - - - - - - -X	60
Communication: Informs the staff of decisions	0- - - - - -X	30
Fair treatment: Has no favorites	0-- - - - - - - - - - - - -X	80
Reprimandations: Reprimands where needed	0X	0

Figure 12-2

Chapter 3, people at different levels in an organization perceive someone else as making most of the decisions.

It is important to know how people feel about how much influence they now have and should have, even though their perceptions of others' influence may not be accurate. The course of action to either change perception or change the situation should be planned only after the data are in.

AMOUNT OF INFLUENCE
(INSTRUMENT II)

Directions to the staff: How much influence do you think each of the following roles now has in the school district? Mark an "X" where the influence now is.

How much influence do you think each role *ought to have* in your school district? Mark an "O" where you think it *ought to be*.

Assurance of anonymity: Mail your response in the enclosed envelope. Do not sign it. Your individual response will not be seen by anyone except the statistical clerk.

AMOUNT OF INFLUENCE

	A little		Some		A great deal		Discrepancy
	0	20	40	60	80	100	
School Board				0 – – – – – – – – – – X			20–
Superintendent			0 – – – – – – – – – – X				20–
Principal			0 – – – – – – – X				15–
Teachers		X – – – – – – – – – – – – – – 0		•			60+
Parents			0X				--
Pupils		0X					--

Figure 12-3

Again, hypothetical scores have been entered to indicate what Tom's school might look like.

Note that it is estimated that the teachers in Tom's school will, like most teachers, perceive that most of the power rests with the hierarchical jobs and that they as teachers have less influence than they should have. In this case, teachers perceived that parents have some influence and should have some. Pupils have little and should have little, according to this hypothetical summary.

These data, as pointed out before, are perceptions. People behave as they perceive things to be. The correction of misperceptions or the modifications of the situation can be planned only after the data are known.

THE PRINCIPAL'S PROFILE

Instrument III

Tom really wanted more information on the precise ways teachers perceived him. Teachers were requested anonymously to mark an "X" on the scale representing the frequency of Tom's behavior for each item. See Figure 12-4.

	Never	Seldom	Sometimes	Usually	Almost Always
Supportive of teachers					
1. Values good teaching					X
2. Encourages initiative of teachers				X	
3. Shares risks with teachers			X		
4. Gives credit to the teachers		X			
5. Helps teachers develop their own style of teaching	X				
Making decisions					
1. Makes decisions by himself					X
2. Carries through on decisions				X	
3. Consults staff before making decisions		X			
4. Will change mind if more data are provided		X			
Obtaining resources					
1. Helps teachers determine need			X		
2. Helps locate materials			X		
3. Facilitates getting materials			X		
Giving sanction					
1. Will review questions quickly			X		
2. Will support good plans				X	
3. Will keep an open mind on suggestions		X			
4. Will say yes or no when a time for a decision				X	
5. Will stick by the teacher if he has given sanction			X		
Operational procedures					
1. Has an open door	X				
2. Makes teachers meeting meaningful		X			
3. Gives time equally to staff	X				
4. Is prompt in response to teachers' requests			X		
5. Has good relationships with parents			X		

Figure 12-4

The ideal profile depends upon the expectations of the group or "the group norms." Again, this is simply hypothetical data about how teachers might have perceived Tom to be. In the area of supporting teachers, they recognize that he values good teaching and that he usually encourages initiative. He doesn't always give credit to the teachers, and he may desert them if they get into trouble.

In the area of making decisions, they perceive him as making them himself and usually carrying them out. They see him as seldom consulting the staff before he makes decisions and as being somewhat stubborn and arbitrary once he has made up his mind.

Obtain resources: He only helps teachers get resources sometimes.

Giving sanction: Again, he is perceived as giving approval to good plans but not keeping an open mind to other approaches or sticking by the teacher after he has given approval.

In the area of operational procedure, Tom's teachers perceive him as not being open or responsive to the teachers. His teachers' meetings are seldom meaningful to teachers.

ANALYSIS OF THE DATA

The first milestone directed Tom to review instruments and select those to be applied by October 10. The second milestone, December 1, called for the data to be gathered, ready for analysis. The supervising director of elementary education had the responsibility for applying the criteria and judging whether or not the milestones were reached, and authorizing next steps according to the milestone plan. He also should have assisted in getting outside resources where needed.

In this case study the author deliberately selected a case which was rather critical in order to demonstrate the use of instruments which point out broad discrepancies. The reader might assume that Tom's case is hopeless and that the director of elementary education should simply recommend dismissal, and use the evidence collected for the basis of his recommendation. This would be the worst thing that could have happened to Tom or to the school district. It would also have put the elementary director in the same mode of behavior as Tom is accused of. It would be a betrayal of the total commitment made to Tom. Tom might well have been in a hopeless situation, but Tom had to be judged upon whether he was reaching the milestones satisfactorily, based solely upon the criteria agreed upon. In this case Tom had reached milestones one and two with courage and was told so. Now was the time he needed encouragement and outside resources.

A skilled consultant was engaged to assist Tom in analyzing the data and determining a course of action. The following emerged.

1. The data were not as discouraging as they appeared. It is the nature of people in an organization to want things to be better. Typically, as things improve expectations increase. Therefore, there tends always to exist a difference between the "ideal" and the "real" as perceived by members of an organization.
2. Tom did have some pluses. He was perceived as having a high value for good instruction. Many principals never achieve this recognition on the part of their staffs.
3. The burden of these instruments was heavily upon the principal to make things "ideal" for the teacher. What were their responsibilities toward the organization and to make things better? Did they also contribute to the adversity of the current situation?
4. Tom showed great courage in selecting these instruments and exposing himself to intensive scrutiny. The risk to his personal ego was high. Unless he was aware of these risks and able to live with them, he should not have engaged in such a procedure and should have taken the inevitable alternative of stepping aside.
5. The worst possible course of action for Tom to pursue would be for him to become defensive and attempt to discredit the findings of the instruments. He must realize that perceptions are perceptions whether or not they are true. People behave always as if their perceptions were true. If sailors believe the world is flat, they simply will not sail very far out! Perceptions are changed only by something which happens to cause one to perceive in a different way.

THE PROBLEMS

Milestone ⚠3 required the identification of problems with the assistance of an outside consultant. These would then be prioritized and a few selected to work on.

The problems were to be stated as institutional or school problems—not as Tom's problems. It was time to change the focus from an individual, albeit a central person, to the total organization.

The problems:

1. A more open system of communication needed to be established so that all staff members could have the information they need to operate most effectively.
2. A plan needed to be devised so that staff members could receive the necessary sanctions and assurances they need to do their work effectively.
3. A plan was needed to assure staff members access to resources they needed for their teaching activities.

4. A clearer understanding was needed of the limitations within which different people in the hierarchical structure must work—the Board of Education, the superintendent, the principal, the teacher.
5. The staff needed to develop cooperative processes to solve problems of the organization.

The consultant advised that a group session was needed to involve the teachers in the selection and solution of problems affecting them and their school. The principal and supervising director agreed. It was therefore planned that one of the two annual inservice days permitted in the district should be used, coupled with a Saturday morning, for a conference on school problems.

The supervising elementary director provided professional growth funds to pay the fee of the outside consultant and to provide meals and a small stipend for teachers so that the conference could be held in a facility outside the school district. The principal would confine his role as chairman to get the conference started, but from then on would participate as a group member delegating the leadership of the conference to the outside consultant.

THE PLANNING CONFERENCE

The principal began the conference by telling the staff that they would have the next day and a half to look at their school and help decide how the *working arrangements* would be improved. Data summaries of the diagnostic findings were displayed on large charts. These were so that they could not be carried away for misuse later. Tom said, "To assist us we have Dan Thomas, a group process specialist. He will take over the leadership of the group and I, as principal, will become a group member. Please call our consultant Dan and call me Tom. Being on a first-name basis should help us communicate better."

Dan, the consultant, told the group to review the data summaries and use them as reference, but not to consider them anything except indicators of problem areas. He then divided the group into small groups of four. Tom was assigned to one of the groups.

Task 1. *Identifying goals*. The task was for each group to list the way things would be next June in staff relationships if things were as "I would like to see them."

One person was to act as recorder for the group. He was to write down each person's idea, regardless of what it was. No negative comment was to be made of any person's ideas.

At the end of 40 minutes, each group posted their total list on large sheets of paper near their work area.

Group One's list looked like this:

By next June:

1. I will feel that my fellow teachers approve of what I am doing.
2. My principal won't get mad at me when I make a mistake.
3. Our teachers' meetings will be interesting.
4. We will have what we need to work with.
5. I can talk to the principal as much as I need to.
6. I'll feel comfortable going into the teachers' rooms.
7. I won't be afraid to make a suggestion.

Task 2. *Agreeing upon goals*. The task was for each group to agree upon three goals and only three, which they would most like to see achieved. After considerable discussion, group one categorized their seven goals under the following headings:

1. My fellow teachers
2. My relationship with the principal
3. Facilitating my work

If these three categories were typical and could be synthesized with those selected by other groups, then the total group would have something to work on. These problems became: (1) the improvement of interpersonal relationships among the teachers; (2) the improvement of interpersonal relationships with the principal; (3) the facilitation of good teaching efforts.

Task 3. *Fixing responsibility*. The task was for the group as a whole to prepare a set of tasks to accomplish each of the above goals. These tasks were to be specific, not general.

Each goal was written across the top of a large chalkboard. Under the goals were drawn four vertical columns with the following headings: What is to be done? Who is to do it? When is it to be done? How will it affect me?

To facilitate thinking, the group leader, Dan, asked the group to take a sheet of paper and line it according to the columns on the board and to do this individually for each of the three problems. The individuals were asked to be *specific*, not general. For example: Instead of saying, "The principal should be available to teachers," say, "The principal should have hours when teachers can see him in his office." Or, instead of saying, "The teachers shouldn't gripe so much," say, "The teachers should confine their remarks to honest expressions of opinion about which something can be done."

Task 4. *The preparation of an overall plan.* This task was to combine the best of the suggestions and agree upon a plan of action.

It was now time to fill in the columns on the chalkboard for the group as a whole. This required a skillful leader, which Dan was, in order to maintain open communication and honest expression of ideas.

The list of a feasible set of suggestions included the following:

GOAL 1. IMPROVEMENT OF INTERPERSONAL RELATIONSHIPS AMONG THE TEACHERS

Suggestion 1. Take a course in interpersonal communications such as that developed by an educational laboratory.

Who? All teachers.
When? This spring.
How will this affect me? I will know my colleagues better and will be more open and supportive of them.

Suggestion 2. Plan the agenda for teachers meetings and hold them only when necessary.

Who? A committee of teachers meeting with the principal.
When? Monthly meetings.
How will this affect me? It will give me a chance to make my suggestions to a committee member.

Suggestion 3. Resist criticism of professional colleagues except in open exchange between the two.

Who? All.
When? At each teachers meeting we should give attention to the professional climate and openness among the faculty.
How will this affect me? I will be assured that I won't be criticized behind my back.

GOAL 2. THE IMPROVEMENT OF INTERPERSONAL RELATIONSHIP WITH THE PRINCIPAL.

Suggestion 1. Invite the principal into our classrooms and discuss our problems with him.

Who? All teachers.

When? At least once before the end of the school year.

How will this affect me? It will give me a chance to test out my ideas and inform the principal of my program.

Suggestion 2. The principal should budget time to visit teachers and discuss their problems.

Who? Tom.

When? He should set aside an hour in the morning to visit classes on invitation, and he should have open office hours toward the end of specified days.

How will this affect me? I will know when I can see the principal.

Suggestion 3. The principal should test his ideas with those affected before making up his mind. He can do this by appointing committees to discuss ideas with him.

Who? The principal.

When? Any time it is necessary to change procedures and create new ones.

How will this affect me? It will be assured that I will have a chance to express my opinion before he makes up his mind about something which affects me.

GOAL 3. TO FACILITATE GOOD TEACHING.

Suggestion 1. Teachers should talk over the feasibility of their plans with the principal to let him know about the needs for supplies and materials before the program is begun.

Who? Each teacher.

When? Before starting a new program in the classroom.

How will this affect me? I will know what I can expect in the way of supplies and material.

Suggestion 2. The principal should help us get the assistance of a subject matter specialist when we need one.

Who? The principal.

When? After the teacher requests it.

How will this affect me? It will assure me of the help of a specialist when I need it.

Suggestion 3. The principal should talk over his criteria before he judges our performance.

Who? The principal.

When? Before he judges our work.

How will this affect me? It will inform me about the criteria he will use for judging my work, and I may be able to influence the criteria if I don't think they are good.

After the two day retreat, as you can imagine, the atmosphere in Tom's school was greatly improved. Teachers began to feel hopeful. They saw him as less of an ogre and as more of a humanist. They also saw that the tasks of improving the working relationships in the school were shared and that each had a responsibility toward its achievement. It was not solely the principal's problem.

Milestone △4, April 1, for Tom was a progress report on the solution of the problems identified, with next steps indicated.

Tom had much to report to his supervising director. He listed each of the three major goals and the three agreed upon suggestions. He reported the progress of each.

He was keeping office hours.

He had already visited ten classrooms at teachers' invitations.

He had arranged for an inservice training course for his faculty in *Interpersonal Communications*. Dan was the group leader. Two-thirds of the staff were enrolled. Tom was a group member.

Tom reported that teachers were less likely to gripe and more inclined to discuss problems openly.

Teachers meetings were being held more frequently. When Tom invited teachers to help plan the meetings, more needs emerged for meetings than had been anticipated. Teachers no longer complained about the meetings, but demanded more of them. Often the teachers meetings were used to discuss potential changes in policies and procedures.

Five subject matter specialists from the central office had visited teachers upon their requests.

Tom had worked over his performance criteria with the assistance of a teachers committee. He had presented these to a teachers meeting.

Tom had also assisted two teachers in getting more appropriate books and materials for their accelerated groups.

Summary, Milestone △5. June 1, was a summary of progress made during the year.

The original goals were reviewed, and progress begun in April had been carried forward beyond normal expectations. The supervising elementary director rated Tom commendable for meeting the milestones on time—and effectively. Tom's potential as a good leader was recognized.

As a next step, Tom indicated that he planned to do some more work to prepare himself better for leadership. The supervising director suggested that Tom do one more discrepancy model to assist himself in selecting the areas in which he needed the most work. See Figure 12-5. They designed the instrument together, and included on one page areas of poetntial work. Tom then listed his perception of how important this area was to him with an "X." He then marked his estimate of his own competence with an "O." The discrepancies would help him decide which areas needed most work and training as a self-improvement program.

SELF-EVALUATION

Functions	Least--	Importance							--Most	
	1	2	3	4	5	6	7	8	9	10
Communications										
Coordination of teaching										
Public information										
Equipment and facilities										
Morale										
Planning										
Policies and procedures										
Contribution to the profession										
Work assignment										
Planning professional growth opportunities										

Figure 12-5

DEFINITIONS

Communication:
    Ability to establish rapport with others and excnange information openly and honestly. Always making others understand clearly and being able to understand others.

Coordination:
> The skill of planning with and for others so that work and human relations fit well together and work in harmony.

Public information:
> The knowledge of the parents' needs for information, and techniques for obtaining support and understanding of school problems.

Equipment and facilities:
> Expertise in the equipment and facilities needed for schoolwork. Knowledge of costs, sources and comparative quality.

Morale:
> A knack for keeping people satisfied in their work.

Planning:
> The skills to define problems, reduce them to parts and plan effective solutions.

Policies and procedures:
> The clear understanding of the district policies and the procedures which have been generated to carry out the policies. The ability to interpret policies and procedures to others.

Contribution to the profession:
> The participation in a professional organization which gives its members an opportunity to improve themselves and also to upgrade their profession.

Work assignment:
> Skill and experience necessary to recruit and assign teaching responsibilities according to the interest and abilities of the teacher.

Planning professional growth opportunities:
> The ability to help teachers plan their own professional growth opportunities and obtain access to existing opportunities.

Self-evaluation, which is assisted by the use of this instrument, helps an individual evaluate his own strengths and weaknesses at any given point in his development. It also helps him survey across a broad spectrum of possible functions—those that he perceives as most important to him.

After completing a self-evaluation survey, the respondent should do something. What he does will depend upon his desire to improve and the opportunities available.

If some action is taken either through self-help, course work, reading or on-the-job activities, the respondent should review his own profile again after a period of time.

In Tom's case, if he decided to take course work during the summer, or read, or join an administrative planning group, then he should reassess his own profile using the same instrument at the end of the experience.

This process has several advantages.

1. He systematically assesses his own needs.
2. He selects those experiences which he believes will help him most.
3. He reassesses his position at the end of the experience.
4. He "takes credit" for those things which he achieves.
5. He eliminates those things which are no longer important to him.
6. He keeps a periodic check on his own professional aspirations, growth and achievements.

SUMMARY

This chapter emphasizes the importance of using accurate information about the school as a total institution when planning changes.

Institutional diagnostic techniques rely heavily upon analyzing the discrepancy between one's perception of the way things are and how one believes they should be. If this discrepancy is too great among most members of an organization, the organization is unhealthy. The closer these two views become, the healthier the institution becomes.

This chapter presents several models of how these instruments can be designed and utilized to gather information about the health of a school organization. These devices are never used to score or otherwise categorize institutions as good or bad. They are always used to gather information for problem solving.

When problems do exist, a plan of action is required. This plan should be precise, designating milestones of achievement for review and spelling out who is responsible for what as well as the criteria for judging whether or not the milestone is reached.

The solution of complex problems regarding the health of an organization often requires the intervention of an outside, "neutral" consultant who can moderate planning of constructive action on the part of many people.

The chapter also contains a description of how to use a self-evaluation discrepancy model to assist an individual in planning his own self-improvement program.

Glossary of Technical Terms

GLOSSARY OF TECHNICAL TERMS

ACCOUNTABILITY SYSTEM. The process selected to hold a person responsible for the actual results achieved by his efforts as against effort or time expended.

ACTIVITY (in flow charting). A necessary process to reach the next event progressively in a series of events planned to reach a goal.

ALTERNATIVE FUTURES FORECASTING. A process used by scholars to prepare alternative descriptions of what the future will be like if certain combinations of events come about. (See SCENARIO.)

AUTONOMOUS UNIT. An independent, self-directing unit within a larger unit of a school district. (See DECENTRALIZATION or DELEGATION.)

BEHAVIORAL OBJECTIVES. Objectives defined in terms of specific criteria, such as:
1. Who the performer is.
2. What he is to do.
3. Where he is to do it.
4. How well he is to do it.
5. Within what period of time he is to do it. (See OBJECTIVE.)

COMPUTERIZED PROJECTIONS. A process utilizing the computer to forecast future economic, social or demographic speculations by projecting data in different combinations and with different variables introduced.

CONSENSUS TECHNIQUES. Procedures for helping groups reach agreement and finally produce a statement with few or no ambiguities. It has a built-in prioritizing element. (See MODIFIED DELPHI.)

COST BENEFIT ANALYSIS. A process for appraising the anticipated benefit of an activity in terms of cost. (See PPBS.)

CRITICAL PATH METHOD (CPM). A process for analyzing alternative ways of reaching an outcome and selecting the best way (critical path) of getting there.

DATA (in decision making). Information. It is important that data have the following characteristics:
1. Accuracy
2. Variety (several sources)
3. Tempered with wisdom and judgment
4. Be subjective as well as objective

DECENTRALIZATION. The process of fixing responsibility and accountability for decision making in various subcenters rather than concentrating all such power in one center.

DECISION-MAKING PROCESS. The systematic consideration of each element which goes into decision making—including weighing alternatives against data and values to select the best approach to problem solution.

DELEGATION. Giving authority to a lower administrative level along with responsibility.

191

DELPHI TECHNIQUE. A process for systematically getting opinions on the likelihood of an event happening and at what future date. A group of experts is polled. Subsequent rounds allow the experts to correct and modify their original opinions and come close to consensus.

DELPHI TECHNIQUE (Modified). Any modification of the Delphi technique which permits participants to correct their original opinions and come close to consensus.

DISCREPANCY MODELS. Any of several instruments which point out differences between the way things are perceived to be and what is desired.

DIAGNOSTIC INSTRUMENTS, ORGANIZATIONAL. Instruments (checklists or preference indicators) which are used to ascertain how people feel about the organization in which they work. (See INSTITUTIONAL DIAGNOSTIC TECHNIQUES.)

ENCOUNTER GROUP. Nonstructured sensitivity training group with face to face interaction among participants. (See SENSITIVITY TRAINING.)

ERIC. The Education Resources Information Center, which provides reference publications through various centers in the United States.

EVALUATION. The process employed to assess the worth of a thing. In education it is usually formalized into a five-step process of:
1. Enumerating goals.
2. Designating information needed.
3. Designing instruments or ways of collecting the data.
4. Identifying discrepancies between what is desired and what exists.
5. Identifying corrective action if needed.

EVALUATION, FORMATIVE. The evaluative process applied along the way to assure good and immediate information to assist in the program or project development.

EVALUATION, SUMMATIVE. The evaluation process applied at the end of a project.

EVENT (in flow charting). A major step on the main flow of a planned sequence. (See FLOW CHARTING.)

FLOW CHARTING. Diagrammatic representation of the sequence of events that go into a process or project.

FORCE FIELD ANALYSIS. A technique for analyzing forces for and forces against any particular set of actions being successful. It is based upon the assumption that any set of conditions is maintained as it is because of the opposing forces which hold it in place.

FUTURES GAMES. A specific technique calling for a group to consider:
1. What conditions will be like at a given point in the future.
2. What skills and attributes will be needed at that time.
3. How the school can best begin to meet these needs now.

GOAL. A target, usually descriptive of a long range program of from one to five years in scope, established as a guide to action and as a basis for generating more precise objectives. (See OBJECTIVE and BEHAVIORAL OBJECTIVE.)

INFLUENCE (in decision making). The power of effect that one person or thing has on another. It is important in decision making because: it can be positive and open; it can be controlling and restrictive; or it can be sought or avoided.

INSERVICE TRAINING. Processes by which educational personnel learn new methods, information or attitudes while on the job.

INSTITUTIONAL DIAGNOSTIC TECHNIQUES. Methods of ascertaining problem areas within an organization. Such information can provide a key to the action necessary to help solve problems in an organization. (See DIAGNOSTIC INSTRUMENTS.)

INTERPERSONAL COMMUNICATIONS. The process by which two or more people make their thoughts known to others and understand the meaning of those with whom they are communicating. The emphasis in such training systems is on understanding, openness, acceptance, clarity of expression, honesty and willingness to influence others and to accept influence from them.

LABORATORY METHOD. A group method for problem solving based upon interaction. (See NTL.)

MATRIX, DECISION. A grid with the people involved indicated on one axis and the decision to be made on another. A symbol for the role of each person in the decision process is entered in each cell. The matrix is used to chart each concerned person's role in decision making, whether he initiates, approves, consults or is simply informed of a decision.

MILESTONES. A predetermined set of achievement points along the route to goal achievement. Milestones are review points at which indicators of progress can be reviewed.

NEEDS ASSESSMENT. A process of determining needs, usually consisting of four steps:
1. Identifying areas of concern.
2. Checking to determine what the situation is at present.
3. Clarifying values and criteria.
4. Listing discrepancies.

NEGOTIATION. The process by which agreement is reached between or among people with conflicting goals or purposes. It usually results in some gain and some loss by each person who holds an extreme position.

NOMINATING TECHNIQUES. A process employed to identify opinion leaders by asking members of the group to list two or three group members whose judgment they trust. A tabulation of those most frequently listed emerges as the recognized opinion leaders.

NTL (National Training Laboratory). An association of training specialists employing group techniques for improving interpersonal understandings and communication skills. NTL also publishes some materials useful to their purposes.

OBJECTIVE. Specific outcomes anticipated as a result of systematic organized managerial or instructional activities. (See GOAL.)

ORGANIZATIONAL DEVELOPMENT. Any set of procedures which are designed to assure that the needs of all elements of an entire organization are met in order to assure functional improvement.

OPINION LEADERS. Persons whose judgment is sought by others in their group. (See NOMINATING TECHNIQUES.)

PARAPHRASING. A process used in perception checking—restating in your own words what the speaker has said without expressing value judgment. (See PERCEPTION CHECKING.)

PERCEPTION CHECKING. A process for checking for meaning or accuracy of understand, usually employing paraphrasing. (See PARAPHRASING.)

PERT. Program Evaluation Review Technique. A systems approach to planning and analyzing progress and steps of a given project. (See SYSTEMS APPROACH.)

PPBS. Planning, Programming, Budgeting System. A technique for determining the benefit from a given amount of resources to the achievement of alternative goals in education. (See COST BENEFIT ANALYSIS.)

PREROGATIVE (in decision making). The right or privilege to make a decision.

PRIORITIZING. A method of determining what should come first in a series and in what order thereafter.

PROCESS ROSTER (in flow charting). A list of essential events to be completed in sequence before a project or process is finished. (See FLOW CHARTING.)

PROCESS TRAINING. Special training programs to teach individuals such processes and skills as ways to communicate more effectively, how to solve problems or how to apply systems analysis. Process training usually applies group techniques of interaction in the training procedure. Usually more structured than open sensitivity training.

PROGRAM ANALYSIS (in PPBS). A seven-step review procedure applied in PPBS to select the most cost-effective alternative to achieve a given goal; including review of:
1. Multiyear goal
2. Measures of effectiveness
3. Alternatives considered
4. Resources required
5. Feasibility
6. District organizational ability to perform the tasks required
7. Multiyear fiscal plan (See PPBS and COST BENEFIT.)

PROXIMITY, PRINCIPLE OF. The theory that the closer a person is to a program or project the more he will favor it. Closeness can be involvement, knowing someone involved, or physical proximity.

RECYCLE. Redoing a thing with modifications after feeding data back into the system.

REGIONAL LABORATORIES. Educational research and development centers which contract with the National Institute of Education and other educational agencies to do systematic educational research and development.

SANCTION. The approval of an administrative course of action by the policy level person or group.

SCENARIO (in future forecasting). A word picture of what conditions will be like if a certain combination of events take place. (See ALTERNATIVE FUTURES.)

SELF-EVALUATION. A process by which a person inventories his strengths and weaknesses in comparison with his ideal. This evaluation helps him determine areas in which he would like to improve.

SENSITIVITY TRAINING. A process of interaction designated to increase a person's awareness of his own and other people's unique qualities. A purpose is to improve a person's ability to communicate his true feelings openly. (See ENCOUNTER GROUP and NTL.)

STAFF DEVELOPMENT. A planned program to improve the staff on the job. (See INSERVICE TRAINING.)'

SUPERVISION. A method used by one person or group to assist another or guide him toward better performance.

SYSTEMS APPROACH. A strategy for problem definition and solution which emphasizes the interaction among problem elements and also between the immediate problem and its larger context. Specifically avoids traditional, independent or ad hoc treatment.

TASK (in flow charting). A specific piece of work which must be accomplished in order to support a major activity in a planning sequence of events. (See ACTIVITY and FLOW CHARTING.)

T-GROUP. A training group used in National Training Laboratory (NTL) sensitivity training. (See SENSITIVITY TRAINING.)

TRIAD TECHNIQUE. A technique including three individuals. Each in turn states a concern while the other two help him clarify his meaning by paraphrasing.

VALIDATION. Any method employed to determine the correctness or truthfulness of a set of assumptions or ideas.

VALUES (in decision making or needs assessment). The things we believe in such as theory, philosophy or general affective goals. Values are used to screen data in decision making and needs assessment.

Index

Index